IS GOD TO BLAME?

MOVING BEYOND PAT ANSWERS

TO THE PROBLEM OF EVIL

GREGORY A. BOYD

InterVarsity Press
Downers Grove, Illinois

InterVarsity Press
P.O. Box 1400, Downers Grove, IL 60515-1426
World Wide Web: www.ivpress.com
E-mail: mail@ivpress.com

InterVarsity Press® is the book-publishing division of InterVarsity Christian Fellowship/USA®, a student movement active on campus at hundreds of universities, colleges and schools of nursing in the United States of America, and a member movement of the International Fellowship of Evangelical Students. For information about local and regional activities, write Public Relations Dept., InterVarsity Christian Fellowship/USA, 6400 Schroeder Rd., P.O. Box 7895, Madison, WI 53707-7895, or visit the IVCF website at <www.ivcf.org>.

Scripture quotations, unless otherwise noted, are from the New Revised Standard Version of the Bible, copyright 1989 by the Division of Christian Education of the National Council of the Churches of Christ in the USA. Used by permission. All rights reserved.

Cover design: Cindy Kiple

Cover image: Alfred Gescheldt/Getty Images

ISBN 0-8308-2394-8

Printed in the United States of America ∞

Library of Congress Cataloging-in-Publication Data

Boyd, Gregory A., 1957-
   Is God to blame?: moving beyond pat answers to the problem of evil
   /
Gregory A. Boyd.
      p. cm.
Includes bibliographical references and index.
   ISBN 0-8308-2394-8 (pbk.: alk. paper)
   1. Theodicy. 2. Good and evil. 3. Spiritual warfare. 4. Theodicy.
I. Title.
   BT160.B664 2003
   231'.8—dc21

                                                                    2003010909 ·

P	17	16	15	14	13	12	11	10	9	8	7	6	5	4	3	2	1
Y	15	14	13	12	11	10	09	08	07	06	05	04	03				

To my covenant brother, dear friend, comrade in the war

and perpetual intellectual sparring partner,

Paul Eddy.

Our endless friendly bantering has produced

much more in my life than fun times.

This book is indebted

to our ten years of wonderful persiflage.

CONTENTS

ACKNOWLEDGMENTS

The ideas and arguments found in this book have been developed in dialogue with a number of people to whom a sincere expression of appreciation is in order. The perpetual debates I've had with my good friend Paul Eddy have greatly helped me refine my thoughts. Moreover, his compulsion for research and willingness to share his findings with me have saved me years of library work. I am forever indebted.

Dialogues I've had with my colleagues at Bethel College, at Woodland Hills Church (St. Paul, Minnesota), and more recently, with lively and challenging participants on the discussion board of my *Christus Victor* website, <www.gregboyd.org>, have been extremely beneficial and fun. Thank you for stimulating debates that have sharpened my thinking on a number of points. Others have helped further my thinking as well. John Sanders's remarkable insight into the Bible and knowledge of history has been very beneficial. Tyler and Chelsea DeArmond have been invaluable in editing this work. Randy Barnhart, Alan Rhodes and Jim Bilbey have also influenced my thinking, especially as it concerns middle knowledge. And my many dialogues with Richard and Gina Patton, who offer a slightly different perspective on just about everything, have stretched me in wonderful ways.

Gary Deddo and the entire InterVarsity Press staff have done an outstanding job and have been a joy to work with. Thank you. I must also extend a word of thanks to George Brushaber, president of Bethel College; Leland Eliason, provost of Bethel Seminary; and Jay Barnes, provost of Bethel College. I appreciate the challenges you have each offered to my views but also your defense of academic freedom that has supported me over the last several years.

Two more people must be mentioned. First, I am blessed beyond words to have a committed, loving wife, Shelley Boyd, who asssists me in ministry, supports my work, encourages my spirit, stimulates my thinking and just plain loves me like crazy. Shelley, how can I express my gratitude to you?

Finally, I am profoundly indebted to my loving father, Edward K. Boyd, who passed away this last December. Though a skeptic most of his life, his persistent questioning challenged me and taught me how to think on my own. One of the greatest joys of my life was seeing this carnal, irritable, hardcore rationalist transformed into a peaceful, godly disciple of Jesus the last ten years of his life. I miss him and look forward to our reunion.

INTRODUCTION
Why Did God Do This?

This is a book about the mystery of why tragic things happen the way they do. So it seems fitting to introduce this book with one of the toughest *why* questions a person can ever face: Why did a woman's precious baby die in childbirth?

MELANIE'S STORY

Several years ago, after delivering a sermon on living with passion, I was approached by Melanie, a distraught middle-aged woman.[1] "I have lost my passion for God and my joy in life," she said. "I used to be a fired-up Christian who poured herself into her faith, but now I feel nothing toward God and I'm always depressed. I used to run marathons, but now I'm a blimp. My husband and I used to be so close," Melanie informed me, "but now we're almost total strangers. Church used to seem so exciting, but now it bores me to death. I used to love to read the Bible and pray, but now I find both laborious and aggravating. I just feel dead!"

Melanie desired the passion I preached about that Sunday. She wanted to know how to come alive again.

After some conversation I learned that Melanie's downward spiral began about four years earlier when she lost a baby in childbirth. As long as she could remember, Melanie had wanted to mother children. She didn't marry till her mid-thirties, so to beat the biological clock she and her husband immediately began trying to have a baby. After three years with no success they discovered that because of a medical condition, it was unlikely they would ever be able to conceive a child. Melanie's extreme disappointment was short-lived, however, for quite remarkably Melanie conceived. "We thought it was a miracle," she told me.

Her pregnancy went forward without incident. But her delivery had tragic complications. The umbilical cord was wrapped around her baby's neck, choking the child to death during the delivery. Their miracle had turned into a nightmare, and their life turned into one tormenting *why* question. Why would God miraculously give them a child, only to take the baby away while coming into the world? Why did this happen to them? Even more tormenting, why was God preventing them from conceiving again? Melanie's biological clock had all but wound down in the four years since the tragedy.

After about two years of struggling with doubt and depression, Melanie and her husband sought answers to their questions from a Bible teacher she knew and respected. The answer they received was consistent with the theology she had grown up with.

"God has a reason for everything," this teacher confidently told her. "There are no accidents in God's providence," he continued. "The Lord gives and the Lord takes away, and you just have to trust that God knows and always does what is best. The hand that smites is also the hand that heals. You just have to trust him."

When Melanie asked what good the Lord might have intended by taking her baby and now leaving her without a child, the teacher suggested there was a lesson she and her husband were to learn from this event. "When the timing is right—and God's timing is always right—and when you've learned what God wants to teach you, perhaps then God will bless you with another child," the teacher intoned. "Or perhaps it's simply not his will for you to have children."

Melanie accepted this instruction as gospel truth. She felt guilty because she had difficulty trusting "God's plan." The fact that her life, including her relationship with God and her husband, was slowly deteriorating intensified her guilt. Melanie had come to me with a question about passion, but at this point in our conversation her request changed. She wanted me to help figure out what lesson God might be trying to teach her. Maybe this would enable her to have a baby and get her life back on track.

A DIFFERENT PERSPECTIVE

My heart broke as Melanie told me her story. "Let me get this straight," I said. "You're supposed to believe that God gave you this strong desire to mother a child and then miraculously set you up to believe he was going to fulfill this desire, only to kill the baby he gave to you?" "Well, yes," Melanie sheepishly replied. I asked, "Does that seem like something a loving God would do? Can you picture Jesus doing that to someone?" Melanie was completely stunned by my reply. She had been under the impression that the perspective of her upbringing and of the teacher she consulted was basically the perspective of all Christians.

"What are you saying?" she asked. I took Melanie's hand and looked deeply into her eyes as I continued: "Melanie, do you really believe that God kills babies to teach parents a lesson? And do you really think that God is now refusing to give you any more children until you learn this lesson—though he won't tell you what the lesson is?" "And the clock is running out, so I need to figure it out fast!" Melanie interjected with a desperate tone of voice.

I began to weep when Melanie said this. I felt such grief for the tormented state her theology had put her in. "Wouldn't a good, wise and loving teacher at least tell you what you're supposed to learn?" I could almost hear the wheels turning in Melanie's brain as her eyes stared into mine for a long moment. Finally, as though confessing a deep sin, Melanie spoke up, this time with a tinge of anger in her voice. "To be honest, I know we're not supposed to get mad at God. And I've been afraid to admit this before because it might further jeopardize God's willingness to give me a baby. But this whole thing makes me mad. I just don't get it!"

Then, like an erupting geyser, Melanie exploded with anger and frustration. She pulled her hands away from mine, threw them up in the air and with a loud voice protested, "God lets irresponsible teenage girls and women strung out on crack have babies, but *I* have a lesson to learn! I mean, we must *really* be terrible people to be disqualified from having kids when the bar is set so low!"

When Melanie was done venting, I said to her, "Given your picture of God, Melanie, I'm not at all surprised that you're finding it hard to have a passionate, loving relationship with him. If I can be perfectly frank with you, what you were told to believe sounds like a sick game. God takes your child and refuses you future children till you learn the lesson you're supposed to learn—but he won't tell you what the lesson is. This doesn't sound like a wise and loving teacher, to say the least. How are you supposed to be passionately living for God when *this* is the picture of God you're trying to live for?"

"Are you saying God didn't do this to me?" Melanie asked.

"I have absolutely no reason to think this," I replied. "The one thing I know for sure is that God is fully revealed in Jesus Christ. When we see him, we see the very heart of God. And everything I know about Jesus leads me to believe that God grieves over this situation even more profoundly than you do, if you can imagine that."

Melanie was all ears as I continued. "When things went wrong in people's lives, whether it was about their physical or spiritual condition or some tragedy that happened to them, I don't recall Jesus ever looking for the hand of God in it. Instead, he had compassion on suffering people and treated them like casualties of war. He expressed God's heart by bringing relief to people's suffering. Melanie, I know the Lord is deeply in love with you, your husband and the child you lost. And now he wants to heal you and restore the abundant life he died to give you."

My words were striking a deep chord. Melanie's rage turned to tears, which in a few moments turned to loud cries. For several minutes she hugged me as she wailed. In between her cries she kept on repeating, "He didn't do this to me? God didn't do this to me?" The picture of God that had tormented Melanie for the last four years and had sucked the passion out of her life was beginning to change.

Of course Melanie and her husband would have many questions that would need to be addressed over time—questions that this book wrestles with. But the foundation for their transformation was being laid. In time, Melanie and her husband would learn to define who God is by looking at Jesus Christ. And though grief for their lost child would remain, they would in time learn to live with passion for Christ once again.

WHAT IS YOUR PICTURE OF GOD?

Our attitude toward God is completely determined by our mental picture of God. Like Melanie, many people have trouble passionately loving and living for God because they have a mental picture of him that inspires anything but passion. Indeed, many people who refuse to believe in God do so because they have a picture of God they find untenable. They assume that believing in God means accepting that he orchestrates the kind of misery Melanie was experiencing. If God exists, they reason, he would be responsible for all the evil in the world. Everything that happens would be the working out of his plan. And since these people can't with integrity accept that, they reject God.

This book offers a very different picture of God. Though it will be new to some, it really is not new at all, for it is rooted in the biblical depiction of Jesus Christ. When someone asked Jesus to show him God the Father, Jesus said, "Whoever has seen me has seen the Father" (Jn 14:9). In essence Jesus was saying, *"I am your picture of God."* Many people construct their picture of God from various philosophical premises or their own life experience. But while philosophical thinking can be helpful and life experiences cannot be ignored, Jesus tells us that our understanding of God should be centered on *him*. This is why the Bible calls him the

"Word," the "image" and the "exact imprint" of God (Jn 1:1; 2 Cor 3:17—4:6; Col 1:15; Heb 1:3).

The foundation for this book—and I believe for Christianity as a whole—is the claim that *God looks like Jesus*. As we will see, Jesus spent his ministry freeing people from evil and misery. *This is what God seeks to do*. Jesus wars against spiritual forces that oppress people and resist God's good purposes. *This is what God does*. Jesus loved people others rejected—even people who rejected him. *This is how God loves*. Jesus had nothing but compassion for people who were afflicted by sin, disease and tragedy. *This is how God feels*. And Jesus died on the cross of Calvary, suffering in the place of sinful humanity, defeating sin and the devil, because he passionately loves people and wants to reconcile them to God. *This is how God saves*.

This Christ-centered picture of God is very different than the one Melanie was encouraged to believe. This God grieves with Melanie, seeks to free her from her pain and endeavors to help her move beyond this tragedy by embracing a future full of passionate living. If we keep our focus on Jesus, we have no reason to assume God put Melanie and her husband through this tragic ordeal. Rather, we have every reason to assume God was and is at work to *deliver* Melanie and her husband from their ordeal.

People who become fully convinced that God looks like Jesus begin to love and are empowered to live for God with a passion they never dreamed possible before—regardless of their life experiences. And when they think this through consistently, they find that this revelation frees them to let go of *why* questions. These questions are almost always unanswerable. But they are not unanswerable because God is so mysterious—his character and purposes are unambiguously revealed in Jesus Christ—rather, they are unanswerable because creation is incomprehensibly complex.

My prayer is that you will (1) discover a passionate relationship with this beautiful God and (2) learn to live effectively in an ambiguous world where *why* questions can rarely if ever be adequately answered.

An Overview of This Book

To become convinced that God looks like Jesus, however, we need to do more than be told to think about God as we would Jesus. We need to address certain questions that arise from this picture of God. Most important, if God didn't put Melanie through her ordeal, who did? If God is all-powerful and was seeking to deliver Melanie from her tragic state, why wasn't she delivered? Indeed, if God is all-powerful, why is his creation filled with the kind of suffering Melanie experienced in the first place? It's all well and good to say that God's *character* is revealed in Jesus Christ, but how do we reconcile this with the biblical understanding of God's *power*? How can God be all-powerful and not always get his way? And how do we reconcile the picture of God as Jesus Christ with the picture other passages seem to paint, especially in the Old Testament?

We first need to examine more fully the biblical basis for the claim that God looks like Jesus. Hence, in chapter one I examine what Scripture says about Jesus and what this implies for our understanding of God. I argue that everything we think we know about God—whether from the Bible, creation, experience or philosophy—must be consistent with the truth that is revealed in Christ.

Next, we'll explore the pervasive Christian assumption that there is a specific divine reason for *everything* that happens. I call this view the "blueprint worldview," for it assumes that *everything* is part of God's great plan, a meticulous divine blueprint. In chapter two I show how this view came about, how it makes it impossible to make sense out of radical suffering in the world, and how it contradicts the view of God we are given in Jesus Christ.

In chapter three I begin to outline an alternative way of understanding God and his relationship to the world, one that is consistent with the revelation of God in Christ. I call this the "warfare worldview." Rather than holding to a meticulous divine blueprint, this view holds that God is at war with forces that oppose his will. Jesus' ministry was all about spiritual conflict. If he is our key to understanding what God is like, we must conclude there is a war zone between what God wills and what sinful people and opposing spiritual forces will. Once we understand this, we can more consistently affirm God's love and compassion in the midst of his warfare against evil.

Understanding why God made free beings goes a long way in answering why evil *in general* is allowed to take place. But it doesn't address the mystery of why *particular* evils happen to *particular* people. It doesn't answer the age old question, "Why me?" Nor does it answer why God seems to miraculously answer prayer sometimes but not at other times. Why does everything in life, including God's interaction with us, seem so arbitrary?

I begin to address this issue by examining the book of Job in chapter four. This profound book doesn't answer these questions, but it does give us perspective: life seems so arbitrary because the cosmos and the war that now engulfs it is so unfathomably complex. We can't possibly understand all the influences that converge to bring every particular event about. In other words, the mystery of evil is more a mystery about fallen creation than about God's character or plan.

In chapters five and six I attempt to show that a creation which includes free agents capable of love cannot be one in which God can guarantee his will is always done. Chapter five explores two aspects that God takes into account in determining what he will do, while chapter six outlines a number of variables that affect what prayer accomplishes in the world.

Having addressed the theoretical question of why evil occurs, in chapter seven we look at the practical issue of how we are to live in its midst. Because our understanding of God is centered on Jesus, we are inspired to resist evil and most forms of suffering as ultimately coming from forces that oppose God. What is more, the Bible offers us hope, peace and confidence as we work with God to accomplish his will.

The final two chapters address objections that can be raised against this Christ-centered warfare worldview. Every theological perspective finds some Scriptures more difficult to integrate than others. Hence, in chapter eight I discuss Romans 9, which is perhaps the strongest and certainly the most frequently cited passage that seems to stand in tension with the view I am advocating in this book. I continue this line of defense in chapter nine as I respond to nine other sets of passages that are frequently used to support the blueprint worldview.

My hope is that this book will help people like Melanie gain a more beautiful, Christ-centered picture of God by helping them understand that God is against, not behind, all the evil in the world. For people not sure about the Christian faith, my hope is that this book will present a picture of God that is more attractive and more believable than other pictures they have been exposed to. It avoids what has for many people been the central objection to accepting the Christian God, namely, the idea that every atrocious event in world history is somehow a result of his plan—his divine blueprint.

THE LIE AND THE TRUTH

The most important aspect of faith is our mental picture of God. The way we actually envision God may not be reflected in the theology we articulate. When asked what we think about God, we may recite all the orthodox attributes—love, omniscience, omnipotence—while entertaining a mental picture of God that is unloving and severely limited. Yet our actual picture of God, not our theoretical knowledge about God, most influences how we feel about him. It's impossible to enjoy a genuinely passionate and loving relationship with God when our mental picture of him doesn't inspire passionate love.

Our picture of God not only influences our emotional response to God, it strongly influences our understanding of everything else in our life. Most significant for the purposes of this book, it influences how we interpret suffering and evil in our life. Does Melanie see the hand of God at work in the death of her child, or does she interpret it in some other fashion? It all depends on her picture of God. It is most biblical and most helpful not to see God involved in the evils in this world but to interpret it in some other fashion.

We will begin by looking at Genesis 2—3, which demonstrate that at the root of everything contrary to God's original design for humanity is a lie about God that causes us to question his character. Following this, we will examine God's answer to this lie: the person of Jesus Christ. All of our thinking about God must begin and end with his revelation of himself in his incarnate Son.

THE SERPENT'S LIE

> *Now the LORD God had planted a garden in the east, in Eden; and there he put the man he had formed. And the LORD God made all kinds of trees grow out of the ground—trees that were pleasing to the eye and good for food. In the middle of the garden were the tree of life and the tree of the knowledge of good and evil. . . . The LORD God took the man and put him in the garden of Eden to work it and take care of it. And the LORD God commanded the man, "You are free to eat from any tree in the garden; but you must not eat from the tree of the knowledge of good and evil, for when you eat of it you will surely die" (Gen 2:8-9, 15-17 NIV).*

The loving prohibition. This is the story of how Adam and Eve, and therefore every one of us, became separated from God. God placed the man and woman in a garden prepared for them. In the center of the garden were two trees: the tree of life, from which the man and woman were allowed to eat, and the tree of the knowledge of good and evil, the fruit of which was forbidden to the man and woman. The inspired author is telling us that at the center of the full life God intends humans to enjoy is a *provision* as well as a *prohibition*. The provision—the tree of life—allows us to share in God's eternal fellowship. But God prohibits taking for ourselves what belongs to God, namely, the knowledge of good and evil.

The prohibition is as much an act of God's love as the provision is, for God knows we can only enjoy the provision when we honor the prohibition. God knows we can only live fully as human beings when we honor his holiness, which means his distinctness from us, his "otherness."[1] And the primary way we honor the difference between us and God is to acknowledge that we are not the ultimate moral judges. He is the one and only "judge of all the earth" (Gen 18:25). Our role as God's creatures is to receive, enjoy and reflect our Creator's love and goodness as we exercise the authority over the earth he entrusted to us. But we can't do this if we try to be wise like God, "knowing good and evil."[2] To fully reflect God's image in the way he intended, we must resist the serpent's temptation to be "like God" in the way God has forbidden (Gen 3:5).

Unlike God, our knowledge and wisdom are finite. We simply are not equipped to make accurate and loving judgments about good and evil. To us, even in an unfallen condition, the complex world is mostly ambiguous. Our experience and perceptions of reality are incredibly narrow. Aside from God's revelation of himself, we are incapable of drawing definitive conclusions about most things, especially the state of people's hearts. But we can (1) trust what God tells us about himself, (2) experience fullness of love and life as we commune with God, (3) walk in humble obedience to him, and (4) exercise the authority he's given to us.

When we go beyond this boundary and try to know what God alone can know, when we try to be "wise" like God, it destroys us. In trying to seize what properly belongs only to God, we lose what properly belongs to us. We forfeit our God-given authority on earth, giving it to Satan (see Lk 4:5-7). Instead of being ruled by divine love, we become oppressed by diabolic power. The "accuser" (Rev 12:10) turns us into accusers rather than lovers.

This is why the Lord warned the man and woman, "in the day that you eat of it you shall die" (Gen 2:17). The warning is repeated throughout the New Testament: we are emphatically told to "live in love" and not judge others (e.g., Mt 7:1-5; Rom 2:1-5; 14:1-23; Eph 5:2; Jas 4:11-12). God wants our life to be one of receiving and giving unsurpassable love. But this requires that we refrain from judgment.[3]

Unlike God, we are incapable of loving and judging at the same time. God therefore placed the tree of the knowledge of good and evil in the middle of the garden as a loving warning. It is the prohibition around which our life with God revolves. It is his way of saying, "Be content with

being my creations. Don't try to be me." The blessed life God wants for
us is centered on our honoring this prohibition, honoring God as holy
Creator, honoring the uniqueness of his wisdom and his role as Judge,
and thus honoring the limited but wonderful domain of responsibility
that is ours.

The lie at the foundation. In the Genesis story the crafty serpent
twisted God's intention. He made it look as if God were less than loving
in forbidding humans to eat from the tree. The serpent made it look like
God was threatened by the forbidden tree.

> Did God say, 'You shall not eat from any tree in the garden'?" . . .
> [T]he serpent said to the woman, "You will not die; for God knows
> that when you eat of it your eyes will be opened, and you will be
> like God, knowing good and evil." (Gen 3:1, 4-5)

The serpent accused God of being untrustworthy and Eve of being
naive. The serpent suggested that God lied to Adam and Eve when he
said they would die from the fruit of the forbidden tree. The accuser said
the real reason God didn't want them to eat of the tree was that God was
afraid of competition—Adam and Eve were being duped by this self-
serving deity. God was protecting his exalted position by keeping the
competition in the dark. The sweet life Adam and Eve had thus far enjoyed, trusting God to meet their needs and fellowshipping with him,
was actually a trick. Their innocence, according to the serpent, was actually part of a devious plan by which God kept humans from becoming
all they could be. They could be, if only they'd take matters into their
own hands, wise like God.

This is the foundation of all sin: the lie that God is untrustworthy, the
lie that God is not altogether loving and that he doesn't have our best in-
terests in mind. Adam and Eve came under the grip of this deceptive picture of God. At that moment they stopped trusting God as their source
of life. Consequently, they saw themselves as deficient. They were no
longer OK simply trusting and obeying their Creator.

Eve subsequently bought the lie that in order to fulfill her life she needed to cross the boundary God had set up. Looking at the forbidden fruit with this lie-induced sense of emptiness, Eve no longer heeded God's loving warning to avoid death. She saw the fruit as "good for food and pleasing to the eye, and also desirable for gaining wisdom," and she ate from the tree (Gen 3:6 NIV).

A faulty picture of God led to an ungodly evaluation that in turn brought about a rebellious action. The lie about God created the illusion that Eve could fill her emptiness by disobeying God. The lie created an emptiness as well as the futile and rebellious means of filling it. A false concept of God, and therefore of herself, gave birth to sinful behavior, which in turn brought about spiritual and physical death (see Jas 1:14-16).

This is not merely an account of what happened a long time ago. It's our own story. Under the bondage of the serpent's lie, we try to achieve through our own efforts what God wants to freely give us. We have a God-shaped vacuum in our hearts that only God can fill. But we try to fill that vacuum through our illegitimately seized knowledge of good and evil. Instead of innocently trusting God to meet our innermost needs, we trust our own assessment of things and our own ability to get the things we deem "good." We live by *our* knowledge of good and evil rather than by trusting our loving God.

The "good" we pursue may be respect, security, religion, ethical superiority, the rightness of our opinions, pleasure and so on. And the "evil" we avoid is anything that challenges the "goods" that have become our source of life. We end up desperately trying to attain a full life from a center of emptiness rather than from the center of abundance, which comes freely from our loving God.

This is what the Bible calls life in the "flesh," or life in "Adam" (see Rom 5:14; 8:8-9; 1 Cor 15:22). It is life separated from innocent communion with God, life lived in judgment rather than love. And its foundation is mistrust of God's character, which issues from a deceptive picture of God. To the extent that the God we envision is less than all-loving, gracious, kind and altogether on our side, we can't trust him with our whole being. To the extent we believe this lie, we block the flow of God's life and love into our innermost being and spend our time trying to fill the vacuum with what we can do and get.

THE TRUTH OF THE WORD

Just as the foundation of all that separates us from God is a false picture of God, so too the foundation of all that restores our innocent communion with God is a true picture of God. So everything hangs on the question, Where do we find the true picture of God? The answer that the Bible unequivocally and emphatically gives is Jesus Christ.

Jesus is the truth that dispels the serpent's lie. The root of the word *truth* in Greek means "not covered." The serpent covered the true God from our minds and hearts, but Jesus removes this covering and reveals to us the real God. He is "the way, the truth, and the life" (Jn 14:6). Similarly, the Holy Spirit is called "the Spirit of truth" because he reveals Christ to all who open their hearts to him. The Spirit manifests the One who "uncovers" the Father (Jn 16:13-14, cf. 2 Cor 3:16-18).

To see how Jesus "uncovers" the truth about God and our life, I will examine two New Testament motifs that reveal Jesus as God's self-revelation. The first concentrates on Jesus as the Word of God, the second on Jesus as the image of God.

Jesus is the Word of God. John 1 is a powerful testimony to the centrality of Christ for our picture of God. John opens his Gospel by saying:

> In the beginning was the Word, and the Word was with God, and the Word was God. He was with God in the beginning. Through him all things were made; without him nothing was made that has been made. In him was life, and that life was the light of men. (Jn 1:1-4 NIV)

Among other things, the concept behind *Word* refers to God's thinking and his self-expression.[4] When God thinks, John is saying, *it is Jesus.*

And when God expresses himself, *it is Jesus*. Notice the singularity of John's claim. Jesus is not one Word among others, as though God had more than one mind and more than one mouth. Rather, *wherever* and *whenever* God thinks and expresses himself, it is Jesus Christ.

Moreover, it has been this way throughout eternity. John emphasizes the fact that the Word is not created. He was "in the beginning with God" and is himself *God*. He has been fellowshipping with the Father from all eternity (Jn 17:5, 24). This means that in knowing Jesus, we are not knowing someone "one step removed" from God. In knowing Jesus we are knowing *God himself*, God in his eternal essence. In seeing Jesus, we are seeing the very heart of God.

In fact, far from being created, the Word is actually the Creator. John tells us that everything was made by the Word, through the Word and for the Word (Jn 1:1-3). Creation exists, in other words, as an expression of God and for the purpose of people knowing God. Creation's purpose is found in Jesus Christ.

John also says that the Word is the life and the light of all people. God wants people to know him and share in his life (Jn 17:3). Whenever and wherever people experience true life and true light, it is Jesus Christ, whether they know it or not (Jn 1:4, 9). Whereas the enemy covered up the true God in a veil of deceptive darkness that brought death, Jesus turns the light on so we can see who God really is. In doing this, Jesus gives life. Indeed, he came to the world that we might once again have the abundant life God always intended us to enjoy (Jn 10:10). He desires all people to share in the eternal love he has with the Father and Spirit (Jn 17:20-26).

God made visible. The glorious significance of seeing Jesus as the Word of God is fleshed out by John:

> And the Word became flesh and lived among us, and we have seen his glory, the glory as of a father's only son, full of grace and truth. . . . No one has ever seen God. It is God the only Son, who is close to the Father's heart, who has made him known. (Jn 1:14, 18)

Picking up a theme that runs throughout the Bible, John tells us that no one has ever seen God's eternal, transcendent nature, for God is Spirit (Jn 4:24). Yet Jesus, who is himself "God the only Son," forever existing in perfect communion with the Father, has made God known. In becoming flesh the invisible God made himself visible. In Christ we *see* the glory of God (see 2 Cor 3:18—4:6; 1 Jn 1:1-3). In Christ the previously concealed God has been unambiguously revealed. In Christ the serpent's lie is dispelled.

The point is powerfully expressed later on in John's Gospel. In chapter fourteen we find Jesus telling his disciples, "If you know me, you will know my Father also. From now on you do know him *and have seen him*" (Jn 14:7, italics added). To know Jesus is to know the Father, and to see Jesus is to see the Father. It's that simple. Philip did not quite get the point, however, so he asked Jesus, "Lord, show us the Father, and we will be satisfied" (Jn 14:8). Jesus responded to him by reiterating his teaching even more emphatically. "Have I been with you all this time, Philip, and you still do not know me? Whoever has seen me has seen the Father. How can you say, 'Show us the Father'?" (Jn 14:9).

This passage answers the question, where do we get our picture of God? And the emphatic answer it gives is, *in Jesus Christ*. As the eternal essence of God expressed in human form, Jesus is the visible representation of the Father. Everything we need to know about God is disclosed in him. In knowing Jesus there is nowhere else and no one else we need to look to in order to learn what God is like. If we are thinking biblically and therefore looking to Jesus (Heb 12:2, see also Col 3:1-4), we never need to ask, "Show us the Father."

The center of Scripture. The wholeness and vibrancy of our relationship with God depends on letting God define himself for us in Christ; we should not try to define God outside of or along side of Jesus Christ. Christ is our center, and everything in life must be viewed in relation to him. Our reading of Scripture must be carried out without looking even for a moment to the right or left of Jesus Christ. The Word incarnate is the fulfillment and complete expression of God's revelation in Scripture.

Jesus himself chastised many religious people of his day who did not accept him as the full disclosure of God and thus the centerpiece of Scripture. "You search the scriptures because you think that in them you have eternal life," he said. But "it is they that testify on my behalf" (Jn 5:39). Hence Jesus rebuked them because they refused to come to him for life (Jn 5:40). The purpose of Scripture, Jesus was teaching, is to bring people to him. The words of Scripture don't have eternal life in and of themselves. They are vehicles to bring people to eternal life only insofar as they point people to the One who is eternal life. Indeed, Jesus went on to tell these people that they did not truly believe in Scripture unless they believed in him. "If you believed Moses you would believe me, for he wrote about me" (Jn 5:46).

A similar point is made by the author of Hebrews:

> Long ago God spoke to our ancestors in many and various ways by the prophets, but in these last days he has spoken to us by a Son, whom he appointed heir of all things, through whom he also created the worlds. He is the reflection of God's glory and the exact imprint of God's very being, and he sustains all things by his powerful word. (Heb 1:1-3)

All previous revelations mediated through words were merely anticipations of the revelation of God mediated through his own Son. The revelation of God in his Son is the pinnacle of God's revelation throughout history. He surpasses all previous revelations in that he alone is the perfect reflection of God's glory and exact imprint of God's very being. He is the one true God directly revealed as God's one true Word. As in the Gospel of John, Hebrews connects the unsurpassable revelatory nature of the Son to the fact that he is the Creator and Sustainer of the world as well as the One for whom the creation exists. He is the source of all things and "heir of all things." All of creation finds its ultimate explanation and fulfillment in Jesus.

Hence, we must never think of the revelation of God in Christ as merely *part* of God's total revelation. Rather, everything before Christ must be read in the light of Christ. All previous revelations are authoritative for the Christian insofar as they anticipate and point to God's definitive revelation in Christ.

In contrast to all previous revelations, Jesus is the full revelation of God's wisdom, a wisdom that had been hidden throughout the ages (1 Cor 1:24; 2:7; Eph 3:9-11; Col 2:3). Moreover, in sharp contrast to all previous revelations, in Christ the "whole fullness of deity dwells bodily" (Col 2:9; see also Col 1:19). All that makes God *God*—the whole *fullness* of his deity—took on bodily form in Christ. All previous revelations of God were partial, but in Christ God is revealed fully. All previous revelations were mediated through writing, but in Christ God is revealed *in bodily form*. Therefore, to see God's Son is to see God himself perfectly reflected, exactly imprinted and fully disclosed.

Transformed by the truth. Just as the lie about God is the foundation for all sin, so too the truth about God, revealed in Jesus Christ, is the foundation for all wholeness. Only the revelation of God in Christ completely dispels all forms of the lie we have been deceived into believing. When our picture of God is built on any foundation other than Jesus Christ—whether a foundation of experience, philosophy or Scripture interpreted apart from Christ—we will be vulnerable to believing a lie about God. We will be eating from our own knowledge of good and evil and constructing a false picture of God on the basis of our own fallible judgments. We will embrace a god that is consistent with our jaded presuppositions and fallible expectations, which keep us in bondage to the serpent's lie. Our understanding of God, ourselves, suffering and every other aspect of creation will be to some extent corrupted.

If we are to know the true God and not some subdivine figment of our imagination, all of our thinking about God must be centered on the One who is *the* way, *the* truth, *the* life, *the* light and *the* Word of God (see Jn 14:6).

THE TRUTH OF THE IMAGE

The image of God. Scripture highlights the centrality of the revelation of God in Christ by calling Jesus "the image of God." The passage that most fully develops this theme is found in Colossians. Here Paul writes:

> [Jesus] is the image of the invisible God, the firstborn over all creation. For by him all things were created: things in heaven and on earth, visible and invisible, whether thrones or powers or rulers or authorities; all things were created by him and for him. He is before all things, and in him all things hold together. And he is the head of the body, the church; he is the beginning and the firstborn from among the dead, so that in everything he might have the supremacy. For God was pleased to have all his fullness dwell in him, and through him to reconcile to himself all things, whether things on earth or things in heaven, by making peace through his blood, shed on the cross. (Col 1:15-20 NIV)

There are three points worth noting about this passage.

• *Transformed by God's icon.* First, as we saw in John and in Hebrews, Paul identifies Jesus as the One in whom the otherwise invisible God is seen. The word *icon* comes from the Greek word for "image" (*eikōn*). Jesus is literally God's icon. He is the One in whom God is seen, known and worshiped. It's idolatrous for humans to make and worship icons of God (see Lev 19:4; 26:1), but it's certainly not idolatrous for us to worship the One whom God himself presents as his icon. Indeed, we only know and worship God fully when we know and worship God's icon (1 Jn 2:23; 5:20). Idolatry takes place when we *don't* allow God to define himself for us in Christ but rather embrace a picture of God on the basis of our life experiences, philosophical speculations or non-Christ-centered interpretations of Scripture.

According to Paul all spiritual transformation is the result of the Spirit removing the veil from our minds and allowing us to see the glory of

God uncovered in the One who is his image, Jesus Christ. In 2 Corinthians Paul makes his case by building on the account in Exodus 34:33-35, where Moses had to veil the brightness of God's glory on his face after he received the Ten Commandments. Paul maintains that, in a sense, the glory of God is still veiled from unbelieving Jews, for "their minds were hardened" and "only in Christ is [the veil] set aside" (2 Cor 3:14). "To this very day," he continues, "whenever Moses is read, a veil lies over their minds," for they cannot see that all Scripture points to Jesus (2 Cor 3:15). This recalls Jesus' teaching that the religious leaders of his day blindly searched the Scriptures for eternal life (Jn 5:39-46).

Paul is in agreement with Jesus, saying, "when one turns to the Lord the veil is removed" (2 Cor 3:16). Christ alone uncovers the true God for us. All who know God through Christ may "with unveiled faces" see "the glory of the Lord as though reflected in a mirror." And as we behold this glory we are "being transformed into the same image from one degree of glory to another" (2 Cor 3:18). In other words, when our unveiled minds behold the radiant beauty of the true God in Jesus Christ, we are transformed into his beauty. As we receive the love of God in Christ, we are transformed into his love. As we fix our eyes on Jesus, we gradually become like Jesus. Our transformation is dependent on the picture of God we embrace in our mind and heart. And the picture God gives us is Jesus. The death-producing effects of the serpent's lie are reversed as we unwaveringly fix our sight on the One who is the truth.

Paul concludes his reflections by noting that the truth of the gospel is still "veiled to those who are perishing," for "the god of this world has blinded the minds of the unbelievers, to keep them from seeing the light of the gospel of the glory of Christ, who is the image of God" (2 Cor 4:3-4). The serpent's deception controls their life. To believers, however, "the God who said, 'Let light shine out of darkness' . . . has shone in our hearts to give the light of the knowledge of the glory of God in the face of Jesus Christ" (2 Cor 4:6). Believers have received a light that the veiled minds of nonbelievers cannot receive. Consequently, believers are enabled to trust God, who is as glorious as the One who is his true image. They are no longer in bondage to the lie of the serpent, for they see who God truly is: Jesus Christ. He is a God who loves them to the point of becoming human and dying a hellish, godforsaken death for them on the cross of Calvary.

• *Summing up creation.* Second, Jesus' role as the image of God is connected to his role in creation. Paul's thinking on this point is in line with what we have already found in John and Hebrews.

Paul says that Christ is "the firstborn over all creation" (Col 1:15 NIV). Scholars almost unanimously concede that the point here is not chronological—as though Christ were literally born first. Instead, Paul is referring to Christ as "primogenitor": the firstborn heir to all creation. Paul explains that "all things were created *by* him and *for* him" and he "is before all things, and in him all things hold together." Christ is the source, sustainer and goal of all creation.

Jesus embodies and sums up the purpose of creation. Through the One in whom the invisible God is seen, the purposes of God are clearly seen. Hence, in Christ we see the ultimate truth of who *God* is, who *we* are and what the *world* is to be. More specifically, in Christ we see that God defines himself as One who is for us, to the point of dying for us on the cross. We see that we are both judged in our sin and reconciled to God by his mercy. The purpose of creation is for God to be God for us, and for us to be a people for God. The One in whom all this takes place and thus the One who reveals all this is Jesus Christ.

• *The image and redemption.* This leads to the third observation about Paul's concept of Christ as God's image. Paul not only connects Christ's role as God's image to creation, he also connects it to redemption. The one by whom and for whom the creation exists is the very same one who died and rose again to reconcile the world to God. In both roles Christ functions as God's image. Indeed, it is clear that for Paul the two roles are simply different aspects of the same thing. For in redeeming a people for himself Christ achieves and manifests the purpose of creation.

Paul says, "in [Christ] all the fullness of God was pleased to dwell, and through him God was pleased to reconcile to himself all things, whether on earth or in heaven, by making peace through the blood of his cross" (Col 1:19-20). Whereas certain false teachers of his day where depicting Christ as one aspect of the display of God's fullness, Paul insists, as we have already seen, that "the whole fullness of deity" dwells in Christ (Col 2:9). No aspect of God's fullness was withheld from the incarnation. All we can and need to know about God is found in Christ, for God fully dwells in and is revealed in Christ. And the central purpose of this complete indwelling was to "reconcile to himself all things": to reverse the separation of the Fall and to consummate the purpose of creation by dying on the cross.

Paul also says that the one who is the image of the invisible God is also "the head of the body, the church" and "the beginning and the firstborn from among the dead, so that in everything he might have the supremacy" (Col 1:18 NIV) In dying and rising again Christ becomes the head, the source, of all who will say "yes" to God's grace, and thus all who will participate in his resurrected life. This is the church, the body of those who are God's redeemed people and who thus manifest God's purpose for creation. The church manifests the truth that God is at work in Christ to reconcile the world to himself (2 Cor 5:19). We witness to the truth that God's goal is to "gather up all things in him" and "put all things under his feet" so that he might be "the head over all things for the church" (Eph 1:10, 22). In doing so, we proclaim the truth of who God is, who people truly are and what the purpose of the world is.

The centrality of Christ's death. I want to emphasize that the central way Christ functions as the perfect image and exact imprint of God is by dying on the cross. To be sure, Christ's entire life manifests the true God. But Christ came primarily to die (Mt 20:28). It was his death that defeated the devil and freed us from his bondage (1 Jn 3:8, see also Eph 1:20-21; Col 2:13-16). It was his death that atoned for our sin and reconciled us to God (Rom 3:25; 1 Jn 2:2). It was his death that manifested the wisdom of God (Eph 3:9-11; see also 1 Cor 2:7-8). It was his death that consummated God's purpose in creation. Therefore, it was Christ's death that most decisively reveals who God truly is.

The cross is the absolute center of God's revelation to humanity and his purpose for creation. It is the paradox around which the world revolves. The cross is the mystery that explains, accomplishes and redeems everything. The fullness of God is most perfectly revealed in his becoming the Godforsaken man dying on a cursed tree (Gal 3:13). God's holiness is most perfectly displayed in his becoming sin for our sake (2 Cor 5:21). God's righteousness is most perfectly revealed when he himself becomes a judged criminal (Is 53:5). God's power is most perfectly displayed in his allowing himself to be crucified at the hands of sinners (Acts 2:23). God's glory is most perfectly revealed in the utter shame of the crucified Messiah (Is 53:3; Heb 12:2). God's beauty is most perfectly revealed in the horror of his executed Son.

The cross is the central way Christ images God. Christ was not an innocent third party who was punished against his will to appease the Father's wrath. Christ is himself God, and he voluntarily took our sin and its just punishment upon himself. Hence his sacrifice does not appease God's wrath; *it reveals God's love*. Even in—especially in—his agonizing death on the cross, Jesus is the exact imprint and perfect reflection of God. In the crucified Christ the truth about God, about us and about the world is most perfectly revealed. For the cross is where reconciliation between God and the world is accomplished.

THE TRUTH OF GOD'S LOVE

Projecting onto God. This breathtaking revelation is opposed to every version of the serpent's lie about what God is like. Under the impact of the primordial deception, the "natural mind" does not expect the omnipotent Creator to look like *this*. Our (fallen) tendency, operating out of our illegitimately seized knowledge of good and evil, is to project onto

God every "good" we think God *ought* to have. For example, in classical Western philosophical tradition, emotional vulnerability is a weakness, so we have projected onto God the attribute of "impassability" (above suffering). All variability is thought to be an imperfection, so God must be "immutable" (above any sort of change). Lack of control is also an imperfection, so God meticulously controls everything.

But we get a vastly different picture of God when we simply allow God to define himself in Christ! In Christ we see God's greatness revealed in his suffering: God suffers out of his passionate love for humanity. In Christ we see God's steadfast loving character revealed in his changeability: the Word *became* flesh (Jn 1:14), the holy One *became* sin (2 Cor 5:21), the One who eternally existed in perfect union with the Father *became* one cursed by the Father (Gal 3:13). And in Christ we see God's omnipotence revealed in his weakness: God achieves his sovereign purpose for creation by dying on a cross at the hands of wicked people.

God is unsurpassable love. The foundational difference between the true image of God and every version of the serpent's lie is that Jesus Christ first and foremost reveals God as unsurpassable love: "God *is* love" (1 Jn 4:8, italics added).[5] As the triune Father, Son and Holy Spirit, God is perfect love throughout eternity. In the person of Jesus Christ, God displays this perfect triune love by inviting us into his own eternal fellowship. No image of God ever devised under the power of the primordial lie has come close to matching the outrageous beauty of the true picture of God we are given in Jesus Christ.

The most fundamental distinguishing characteristic of every false picture of God is that it qualifies and compromises the truth about God's love. The most fundamental distinguishing characteristic of the true God is that the love he is and the love he gives is *unsurpassable*. A greater love simply cannot be conceived.

The love that God eternally is, is manifested in the love that God gives. And the love God gives is displayed most perfectly on the cross. "We know love by this," John tells us, "that [Jesus] laid down his life for us." (1 Jn 3:16). "God so loved the world," he says elsewhere, "that he gave his only Son, so that everyone who believes in him may not perish but may have eternal life" (Jn 3:16). In the words of Paul, "God proves his love for us in that while we still were sinners Christ died for us" (Rom 5:8). *This* is what true love looks like. For this is what God looks like.

When he prays to his Father, Jesus connects the love that God is and the love that God gives with his purpose for creating the world:

> I ask not only on behalf of these [the disciples], but also on behalf of those who will believe in me through their word, that they may all be one. As you, Father, are in me and I am in you, may they also be *in us,* so that the world may believe that you have sent me. The glory that you have given me I have given them, so that *they may be one, as we are one,* I in them and you in me, that they may become completely one, so that the world may know that you have sent me and have *loved them even as you have loved me.* . . . I made your name known to them, and I will make it known, so that *the love with which you have loved me may be in them, and I in them.* (Jn 17:20-23, 26, italics added).

God's goal for creation, we see, is for the perfect, eternal love of the Father and Son to be replicated to people and among people. The same eternal love the Father has for the Son is given to all who will receive it. The "glory" that is eternally shared by the persons of the Trinity is given to all who will say yes to it. The unsurpassable love of the Trinity embraces all who will be embraced by it. And in embracing people, this eternal, unsurpassable love is replicated among people.

The ultimate goal of creation, in other words, is for people to receive, replicate and offer back to God the perfect love that God eternally is. We are to be mirrors of his eternal, triune love. We are to become one in love, *just as* the Father and Son are one. Indeed, we are to become one in love by *participating in* the perfect loving oneness of the Father and Son. We are to become "completely one" as we live in the loving oneness of the triune God. We participate in the eternal, triune fellowship and thereby glorify the triune fellowship.

This invitation is not extended to us because we deserve it. To the contrary, left to our own fallen state we are utterly opposed to fellowship with God. In our fallen state we are under God's wrathful condemnation, dead in our sin (Eph 2:1-5). By God's mercy and transforming grace alone we are able to receive God's love and offer this love back to God and others. Only by grace are we enabled to participate in the loving fellowship that God eternally is. This invitation extended to us on the cross and activated through the inner working of the Holy Spirit reveals the unexcelled perfection of God's love. That God goes to this unthinkable extreme to allow undeserving sinners to join in his triune fellowship manifests the unsurpassable love that God is. Again, a greater love simply cannot be imagined.

The crucifixion reveals God's attributes. By dying on the cross Christ displayed God's love and did all that was necessary for us to participate in God's love. He dispelled the serpent's lie and unveiled the truth of who God truly is: unsurpassable love. He did this while defeating Satan, freeing us from Satan's bondage, atoning for our sins and thus opening up the door for us to participate in the very love he was revealing.

Now we more fully understand how the fullness of God was perfectly revealed through a godforsaken man dying on a cursed tree. For the fullness of God is most fundamentally the fullness of his eternal, triune love. Now we understand how God's holiness was perfectly displayed in his becoming sin for our sake (2 Cor 5:21). For the essence of God's holiness is his eternal triune love. Now we understand how God's righteousness was perfectly revealed in his becoming a judged criminal on our behalf. For God's righteousness is simply the justice of his unsurpassable love. Now we understand how God's power was most perfectly displayed in his allowing himself to be crucified at the hands of sinners. For God's power is simply the power of his love. Now we understand how God's glory was most perfectly revealed in the utter shame of the crucified

Messiah. For God's glory is most fundamentally the radiance of his incomprehensible love. And we now understand how God's beauty is most perfectly revealed in the horror of his executed Son. For God's beauty is nothing other than the magnificence of his love put on display.

CONCLUSION

Jesus is the perfect expression of God's thought, character and will. He is God's self-definition to us. We have seen that in Christ, God defines and expresses himself as a God of outrageous love. He is for us, not against us. God also defines humans as undeserving people with whom he is nevertheless in love. *This* is the Word and image of the true God.

Our understanding of God, ourselves and the world cannot be derived from our experience, our independent philosophizing or even our interpretation of the Bible apart from Christ. If we take our cue about these things from any source other than Christ, we will stay under the bondage of the serpent's lie—we will misconstrue God, ourselves and the world. Our picture of God must be centered unequivocally and unwaveringly on Jesus Christ. But this is not always easy to do.

To finite beings like ourselves, the world is ambiguous in the best of conditions. When the child we miraculously conceived dies in childbirth, when the cancer we thought had been cured returns, when terrorists kill thousands in a collapsed skyscraper, when we lose all our possessions in a fire, when we fall once again into our destructive addiction or even when we read about God destroying entire people-groups in the Old Testament, it's easy to let our eyes wander off of Jesus Christ and to begin once again to concoct a god of our own imagining. In the war zone we presently live in, a world that is still under the influence of Satan, "the god of this world" (2 Cor 4:4), things often appear as a raging sea of ambiguity. We need something—Someone—we can anchor ourselves to. The anchor God gives us is Jesus Christ. This alone is what we can trust: God is decisively revealed in Jesus Christ.

Precisely in times like these we must remain "rooted and grounded in love" (Eph 3:17) by allowing Christ to "dwell in [our] hearts through faith." In times like these we must ask God to give us "the power to comprehend . . . what is the breadth and length and height and depth, and to know the love of Christ that surpasses knowledge, so that [we] may be filled with all the fullness of God" (Eph 3:18-19). It is precisely in times like these that we must fix our eyes on "Jesus the pioneer and perfecter of our faith, who for the sake of the joy that was set before him endured the cross, disregarding its shame" (Heb 12:2).

Amidst the sea of ambiguity we swim in, we must not rely on our own "knowledge of good and evil" to figure out what God is like and what he is up to. We must rather "take every thought captive to obey Christ" as we "with unveiled faces [see] . . . the glory of God in the face of Jesus Christ" (2 Cor 10:5; 3:18; 4:6). He and he alone is the one true Word and image of God.

EVIL AND THE BLUEPRINT

When our picture of God is centered on Christ, we are able to avoid the conclusion that God is mysteriously behind all the suffering and evil in the world. Before I develop this thesis further, however, we must confront this unbiblical view. Since the time of Augustine (5th century A.D.) this way of thinking has been widespread within the church.

I call the perspective that supports this understanding the "blueprint worldview," for it asserts that directly or indirectly everything in world history follows a meticulous divine blueprint. This view is succinctly expressed in the maxim "There is a reason for everything." The ultimate reason why anything happens is that God decided it was better to have it happen than not.

There are a wide variety of ways the blueprint worldview gets worked out and defended. Some emphasize God's unilateral control of the world and thus maintain that all events, including human decisions, unfold exactly as God wills. In this view God *ordains* all that comes to pass. This is the "strong" form of the blueprint worldview.

Others grant that humans (and perhaps angels) have free will and thus make choices that God does not ordain. Yet they hold that before the creation of the world God decided to allow (or prevent) every free decision on the basis of whether it contributed to a greater good. This is the "weak" form of the blueprint worldview. Nevertheless, as in the strong form, there is a divine reason for everything. At the very least it can be said that each event in world history happens because God willed not to prevent it.[1]

To confront this traditional perspective I will first outline the two basic lines of reasoning that have led people to it and demonstrate how pervasive this view has been in the theology and life of the church. Next, I offer a critique of the blueprint worldview in the light of God's self-revelation in Jesus Christ. Then, I conclude by offering a brief philosophical critique of this perspective. This will pave the way for developing a Christ-centered warfare understanding of suffering and evil.

THE PHILOSOPHICAL BASIS OF THE BLUEPRINT WORLDVIEW

Basically, there are two lines of reasoning that have led people to the conclusion that everything happens as part of a divine plan. First, many theologians have assumed that if God is all-powerful, which the Bible clearly teaches (e.g., 1 Chron 29:11; Jer 32:17; Mt 19:26; Rev 1:8; 19:6), nothing in his creation can ever thwart his will. At the very least, it is reasoned, God always has the power to stop something from happening if he wants to. Hence, whatever happens does so because God wills it to happen—at least to the point of not willing to stop it. Moreover, if God is all good, which the Bible also clearly teaches (Deut 32:4; Hab 1:13; 1 Jn 1:5), his will must be perfectly good. From this it follows that all that happens in history, however horrendous it may appear, must at least indirectly contribute to the overall good that God wills.

Second, early in church history many theologians accepted a view of divine perfection that was heavily influenced by Hellenistic (Greek) philosophy.[2] Plato and other ancient Greek philosophers assumed that all change is either for the better or the worse, but a perfect being cannot be improved on or worsened. Therefore, God cannot change in any respect. This has traditionally been called "the immutability of God."

For many theologians the immutability of God means that he does not experience time because time is simply the measurement of change. Thus God must experience the world in a "timeless" fashion, an eternal present moment.[3] The immutability of God also means that he is never affected by anything in the world, for to be affected by something outside of oneself is to be changed.

Therefore, in the blueprint worldview God never really *responds* to events in time. How could he if his experience of the world is timeless? There is no "before" and "after" with God—he can't *first* experience something and *then* respond to it. For the same reason, the immutability and timelessness of God is usually thought to entail that God is impassible: he never experiences emotions and never suffers. How could he if he is eternally the same, if nothing ever affects him and he never responds to us?

Even God's knowledge of the world can't be determined by the world, according to many theologians in the blueprint tradition. This would imply that God is affected by something outside of himself. Rather, in this view, God knows everything by knowing himself as the timeless cause of everything. Therefore, God knows world history in a timeless manner because he knows himself as the One who wills world history in a timeless manner.[4]

Of course, Christian theologians who espouse the blueprint worldview find various passages in the Bible to support their view. (I discuss the most important passages in chapters eight and nine.) But their reading of the Bible is rather selective and is strongly influenced by a Hellenistic preconception of what God and his relationship to the world must be like.

Despite their insistence that God is the ultimate cause of all things, virtually all theologians in the blueprint tradition maintain that humans and angels are morally responsible agents. Even theologians who hold that God ordains everything that comes to pass insist that agents are nevertheless morally responsible for choosing what God ordains them to do.

At the end of this chapter I argue that the two lines of reasoning which led to the blueprint worldview are faulty. But first we need to examine the extent to which this worldview has pervaded the thinking and life of the church throughout its history.

THE BLUEPRINT WORLDVIEW IN THE THEOLOGY OF THE CHURCH

The assumption that there is a specific divine reason for every event that takes place has been taught by some of the church's chief theologians. For example, Augustine of Hippo, perhaps the most influential theologian in church history, wrote: "The cause of things, . . . which makes but is not made, is God."[5] And again, "the will of the omnipotent is always undefeated."[6] Many theologians believe this means that nothing ever thwarts the will of God. On this interpretation, even the most horrendous events and most evil deeds are in line with God's sovereign will.[7]

Augustine at one point encouraged Christians who had been victimized by others to find consolation in the knowledge that the perpetrators could not have harmed them unless God empowered the perpetrators and allowed them to do it for a greater good.[8] Indeed, just as Melanie's teacher had done, Augustine went so far as to suggest that when "beloved children" die, God is either teaching the parents a lesson or punishing them or their child for sin.[9]

Calvin at times seemed to reflect a similar blueprint perspective. For example, he wrote:

> Suppose a man falls among thieves, or wild beasts. . . . Suppose another man wandering through the desert finds help in his straits. . . . Carnal reason ascribes all such happenings, whether prosperous or adverse, to fortune. But anyone who has been taught by Christ's lips . . . will look farther afield for a cause, and will consider that all events are governed by God's secret plan.[10]

It seems that for Calvin, God's "secret plan"—his divine blueprint—is unfolding in every event of our life. Nothing happens by chance or simply because people willed it to happen. The *final* explanation for every specific event is "God willed it so." When cancer strikes, when a loved one leaves or when a child is kidnapped, we need look no "farther afield for a cause" than God's "secret plan."

Blueprint theology in worship. Blueprint theology is reflected in some of the church's most beloved hymns. Consider, for example, William Foster Lloyd's famous hymn "My Times Are in Thy Hand."

> My times are in thy hand
>> Whatever they may be
> Pleasing or painful, dark or bright
>> As best may seem to thee.
> My times are in thy hand
>> Why should I doubt or fear?
> My Father's hand will never cause
>> His child a needless tear.

However "pleasing or painful, dark or bright" an episode of our life may be, this hymn seems to encourage us to believe they are caused by our "Father's hand." And if our eyes are full of tears, this hymn seems to reassure us that they are not "needless." They are brought about by God for a good and loving reason.

Similarly, consider Karolina Sandell's famous hymn "Day by Day and with Each Passing Moment."

> The protection of his child and treasure
> Is a charge that on himself he laid
> As thy days, thy strength shall be in measure
> This the pledge to me he made . . .
> Help me, Lord, when toil and trouble meeting
> E'er to take, as from a father's hand
> One by one, the day, the moments fleeting
> Till I reach the promised land.

As with the former hymn, Sandell's hymn can be interpreted as encouraging us to accept "as from a father's hand" every aspect of the "toil and trouble" we meet in life. God promises to protect his children, and so we might conclude that nothing can happen to us that he does not ordain, or at least allow for our own good. In this view if God wanted to protect Melanie's baby (see the introduction), he would have. Since the child died, Melanie and her husband must accept this as coming "from a father's hand" for their own good, as their Bible instructor encouraged them to do.

Blueprint theology in Christian poetry. Throughout history the blueprint worldview has been expressed in poetry written by Christians. Consider, for example, a portion of William Cowper's famous poem "God moves in a Mysterious Way."

> Judge not the Lord by feeble sense
> But trust Him for His grace.
> Behind a frowning providence
> He hides a smiling face.

The logic behind this poem is straightforward. If we assume that the omnipotence of God means God's will is never thwarted in any sense, then everything that happens must in some way reflect his will. And if something is willed by God, it must somehow please him. In this sense God must "smile" at every specific event that takes place. If it had pleased God to prevent an event, he would have done so. Though the universe may seem to "frown" on us at times—as when our baby dies in the birthing process—this poem can be understood as encouraging us to see God's smiling face hiding behind it.[11]

The blueprint response to tragedy. We can also discern the vast influence of blueprint theology in the way many Christians respond to tragedy. The blueprint counsel Melanie received regarding her tragedy is widespread.

Here are some real-life examples of blueprint counsel. Several years ago the little boy of a woman I know was killed by a drunk driver. Before too long, several well-intentioned Christians reassured the distraught mother that "God has his reasons" and that "God is still in control"—as though the drunk driver was actually carrying out the will of God! Similarly, a number of years ago another woman I knew was diagnosed with a fatal blood disease. She already had been suffering for years from an excruciating nerve disorder. In a sincere attempt to comfort her, some of her fellow church members assured her that "God knows what he is doing" even though we can't understand it, for "his ways are not our ways." The woman wondered out loud to me what good purpose God could possibly have for afflicting her in this fashion.

Along the same lines, several years ago I read a front-page newspaper report of what a father said at the funeral of his five young children. Several days earlier all his children had been brutally murdered by his wife. After reciting a brief, gut-wrenching eulogy for each child, the father concluded, "If the Lord giveth and the Lord taketh away, he has given and taken away my children. He gave me them for a short time, and now he has taken them." The man was trying to accept that God was somehow directly involved in what his wife did to his children.

Finally, many of us heard the blueprint worldview expressed in various ways after the 9/11 terrorist attack on America. Some religious spokespersons publicly claimed God was punishing America because of its sin—some pointing at abortion clinics, others at homosexuals and still others at the ACLU or similar liberal groups. Other spokespersons more wisely refrained from such specific speculations but nevertheless tried to assure us that the victims of this tragedy did not die in vain, because, as one leader put it, "there are no accidents in God's providence." Along these lines, John Piper wrote in response to the September 11 tragedy:

> How God governs all events in the universe without sinning, and without removing responsibility from man, and with compassionate outcomes is mysterious indeed! But that is what the Bible teaches. . . .

From the smallest thing to the greatest thing, good and evil, happy and sad, pagan and Christian, pain and pleasure—God governs them all for his wise and just and good purposes.[12]

The point, clearly, is that we must accept the attacks on the World Trade Center and Pentagon as part of God's "wise and just and good" plan.

For some people the assumption that God allows tragic events for a specific divine reason has understandably produced rage. Several years ago a local newspaper interviewed a mother whose daughter had been raped and murdered by a recently released prisoner. Among other things, the mother said, "I've never forgiven God for what happened to my precious child"—as though the criminal who actually raped and murdered her daughter was an instrument God used to carry out his will. If the blueprint worldview is assumed to be true, it's hard to argue that the mother's bitter perspective was mistaken.

As I mentioned earlier, all those who express the blueprint world-view also want to affirm that people are morally responsible for what they do. Of course, all would agree that a mother should not kill her children, that terrorists shouldn't blow up buildings, and that men should not rape and murder young women. Yet, because of the subtle influence of the blueprint worldview, the appeal to the morally re-sponsible choices of people is often not considered the ultimate expla-nation for why things happen the way they do. Rather, the ultimate explanation is found in the sovereign will of God. If God *wanted* things to go differently, it is reasoned, they *would have* gone differently. "The will of the omnipotent is always undefeated"—even when a mother takes the life of her five children, and even when terrorists drive planes into skyscrapers.

Even though the blueprint worldview has a long history and is en-trenched in the life and thought of many Christians, there are a number of things about this perspective that should give us pause. In what fol-lows I offer two sets of criticisms. The first centers on the compatibility of the blueprint worldview with the picture of God we get from Jesus Christ. The second centers on philosophical difficulties that accompany the blueprint perspective.

JESUS AND THE BLUEPRINT WORLDVIEW

All of our thinking about God, ourselves and the world must be singularly focused on Christ. When we focus on Christ, I submit, we arrive at a very different understanding of God, ourselves and the world than what is expressed in the blueprint worldview.

The cross and free agents. To begin, Scripture depicts Jesus' death and resurrection as an act of war. On the cross and through the resurrection, God was overthrowing sin and the devil (Rom 8:3; Heb 2:14; 1 Jn 3:8; cf. Col 2:13-15). God went to the unfathomable extreme of dying a Godforsaken death on the cross because the world was *not* in accordance with God's will. And he did this in order to accomplish God's will, which is to reconcile the world to himself and reconcile humans to each other (2 Cor 5:18-20; Eph 2:13-14). This warfare motif has meaning only if God's will can be thwarted to some degree by free agents. Precisely because fallen angels and humans have rejected God's will for themselves, God went to the extreme measure of dying on a cross.

The cross refutes the traditional notion that omnipotence means God always gets his way. Rather, the cross reveals God's omnipotence as a power that empowers others—to the point of giving others the ability, if they so choose, to nail him to the cross. The cross reveals that God's omnipotence is displayed in self-sacrificial love, *not sheer might*. God conquers sin and the devil not by a sovereign decree but by a wise and humble submission to crucifixion.[13] In doing this, the cross reveals that God's omnipotence is not primarily about control but about his compelling love. God conquers evil and wins the heart of people by self-sacrificial love, not by coercive force.

This leads to another conflict between the revelation of God on the cross and the blueprint worldview. The cross reveals the unsurpassable nature of God's eternal love. It reveals the extreme to which God will go to extend his love to undeserving humans. It lays naked God's heart toward every human (1 Tim 2:4-6; 1 Jn 2:2). But it is difficult to reconcile this picture of God with the picture of God "smiling" at the nightmarish atrocities that sometimes happen to people. If God's heart toward a mother and her twelve-year-old girl is revealed in the outrageous love expressed on Calvary, it is difficult to accept that the girl's rape and murder were also God's will. The cross reveals that God stands *against* all such unloving deeds, not *behind* them.

The cross and the nature of God. The traditional, Hellenistically influenced model of divine perfection stipulates that in every respect God must be unchanging. But this maxim does not square with what the cross reveals about God. How can we hold that God is unchanging when in Christ we see that the second person of the Trinity became a man? "The Word was *made* flesh" (Jn 1:14, italics added). Indeed, how can we assert that God never changes when the cross teaches that the holy One *became sin* for our sake (2 Cor 5:21; see also Is 53:4-6)? If God is willing to participate in something antithetical to his holy nature (sin), he clearly is capable of significant change.

For the same reason it's not clear why we should think God is timeless. For in Christ we discover that God participates in and experiences our time. If the biblical narrative itself wasn't enough to convince us that God genuinely experiences a "before" and "after"—though the entire narrative presupposes this—his taking on human nature certainly should be. God wasn't incarnate before Jesus was born. The Word of God *became* a human baby, *grew up* to be an adult man, *entered* into suffering, and *took upon himself* our sin. To question God's experience of time by postulating that God really experiences all of history in a timeless fashion is to question the authenticity of the incarnation.

When we focus on Christ as our picture of God, it's not clear why we should hold that God is impassible. In contrast to the blueprint view of God, Christ reveals that God is deeply affected by us, passionately responds to us and suffers incredibly for and because of us. Our sin so *affects* God he was willing to experience our sin and punishment to redeem us. He *responds* to our desperate, fallen condition by becoming human and dying for us. He *suffers* for us and because of us. He endures our judgment and is raised from the dead on our behalf. Hence, it seems that any assertion that God is "too exalted" to be genuinely affected by and responsive to us or to genuinely suffer for us should be judged as not sufficiently centered on Christ.

We must allow Christ to define what it means to see God as exalted. And the center of Christ's revelation of God is the cross. God is exalted as he is murdered on a cross. God's sovereignty is revealed in his allowing us to crucify him. God's holiness is revealed in his willingness to take on our sin. God's glory is revealed in the shame of the cross. God's unchanging character is revealed in his ability and willingness to become what he wasn't and to suffer that which is antithetical to himself. The cross reveals that God's deity isn't the absence of change but the perfection of change motivated by love. God is not "above" suffering or being affected and responsive. God is God precisely in his willingness to be affected, to be responsive, and to suffer for the sake of love.

Jesus' attitude toward the afflicted. The picture of God we get from his Word is centered on but isn't restricted to the cross. Jesus' entire life reveals who God is. What we learn about God from the ministry of Jesus, I submit, contradicts the blueprint worldview just as the cross does. Jesus' entire ministry presupposes that God's will is *not* being uniformly carried out in the world. For the sake of brevity, I will examine one chapter of the Gospel of Luke to illustrate this point.[14]

In Luke 13 Jesus discusses Pontius Pilate's murder of a number of Galileans. Jesus asked his Jewish audience, "Do you think that because these Galileans suffered in this way they were worse sinners than all other Galileans?" (v. 2). He was confronting the common blueprint assumption that there is a divine reason for every particular event, including bloody massacres. As in many instances of suffering, people surmised that God was punishing these Galileans for their sins.

Jesus responded to his own question, "No, I tell you; but unless you repent, you will all perish as they did" (v. 3). Jesus rejected the assumption that God was behind every event. More specifically, he rejected the idea that people could discern the disciplining hand of God in evil events. Rather than speculating on such matters, Jesus instructed his audience to concern themselves with their own relationship with God.

Jesus then emphasized the same point by drawing his audience's attention to eighteen people who had recently been killed when the tower of Siloam fell on them: "Do you think that they were worse offenders than all the others living in Jerusalem?" (Lk 13:4). In typical blueprint fashion, some in his audience were interpreting this tragedy as coming from the hand of God. Jesus again rejected the perspective. "No, I tell you; but unless you repent, you will all perish just as they did" (v. 5). As with the earlier question, Jesus rejected the blueprint worldview by invalidating the questions that arose from it. We learn from these episodes that we are asking the wrong question when we ask, "Why did God have this tragedy happen?" or "Why is God punishing these people?"

Shortly after these teachings Jesus confronted a woman who "was bent over and was quite unable to stand up straight" (Lk 13:11). She had been afflicted with this deformity for eighteen years. Jesus didn't offer the counsel that many believers today offer. He didn't suggest that this woman's affliction was somehow part of his Father's "secret plan." He didn't encourage her to accept her affliction as coming from "a father's hand." Neither did he encourage her to believe that the Father was hiding a "smile" behind the "frowning providence" of her deformity.

To the contrary, Jesus taught his audience that this infirmity was the work of Satan, who was resisting God's will. He then demonstrated the Father's will by opposing Satan and miraculously healing the woman (Lk 13:12-13, 16). According to Jesus, God's will was to heal this woman, not afflict her.

This is what we find throughout the Gospels. Without exception, when Jesus confronted the crippled, deaf, blind, mute, diseased or demon possessed, he uniformly diagnosed their affliction as something that God did *not* will. Often Jesus or the Gospel authors specify that it was evil forces (Satan or demons), not God, that were causing the afflictions (Mk 9:25; Lk 11:14; 13:11-16; see also Acts 10:38).

Not once did Jesus suggest that a person's afflictions were brought about or specifically allowed by God as part of a "secret plan." Nor did he suggest that some people suffered because God was punishing them or teaching them a lesson. He didn't ask people what they might have done to get in the sad predicament they found themselves in—even when dealing with demonized people. Jesus never suggested that a person's suffering was brought about to contribute to a "higher harmony." To the contrary, Jesus consistently revealed God's will for people by *healing them* of their infirmities![15]

Peter later summarized Jesus' ministry by telling people Jesus went about "healing all who were oppressed by the devil" (Acts 10:38). Indeed, the central reason Jesus came to earth was "to destroy the works of the devil" (1 Jn 3:8; see also Heb 2:14). This doesn't imply that Jesus and the Gospel authors understood all infirmities to be *directly* caused by Satan or by demons. But it does imply that the ultimate reason for such infirmities is that *God's will is not the only will that determines matters.* The New Testament depicts evil forces and human agents as having a good deal of "say" in what transpires. And tragic afflictions are understood to arise from *these* wills, *not* God's.

In sum, far from revealing that everything follows the will of the Father, Jesus' teaching and ministry reveal a war zone between God and humans and spiritual agents who oppose him. Ultimately, the reason Jesus came to earth and died on the cross was to end this war. Through his life, death and resurrection, and now through the actions of those who believe in him, Jesus is seeking to "destroy the works of the devil." In sharp contrast to the blueprint worldview, Jesus reveals that we shouldn't accept infirmities and other tragedies as coming from the Father's hand. In faith we should resist such things as ultimately coming from wills other than God's.

If Jesus is our picture of God, if we accept his teaching that to see him is to see the Father (Jn 14:9), if we accept that he is the Word, image, form and exact imprint of God (Jn 1:1; Phil 2:6; Col 1:15; Heb 1:3), then we must conclude that much of what transpires in this world is against God's will. Rather than accepting it as coming from the Father, we ought to resist it in the power of the Father.

Does God cause blindness? Some defenders of the blueprint world-view appeal to one episode in the Gospel of John as proof that Jesus saw illness as part of God's plan. In John 9 Jesus and his disciples come upon a blind man. In typical blueprint fashion his disciples ask him, "Who sinned, this man or his parents, that he was born blind?" (Jn 9:2). As was the case with the Jewish audience in Luke 13, the disciples assumed that God must be behind this man's blindness.

Jesus' reply may initially sound as if he were agreeing with this premise: "Neither this man nor his parents sinned." Jesus continues, "He was born blind so that God's works might be revealed in him" (Jn 9:3). Was Jesus agreeing that God intentionally made this man blind? In most translations it may seem so (though even in these translations the "work of God" is revealed in the *healing* from blindness, not in the blindness itself, vv. 4-6). In the original Greek, however, Jesus does not say, "*he was born blind so that* the works of God might be revealed in him." Jesus simply says, "*let* the works of God be revealed in him."

Translators supply the words "he was born blind so that" because they think it is *implied* in Jesus' answer to the disciples' question. And if we assume that Jesus was intending to answer the disciples' question about why God made this man born blind, they have a point. The grammar allows for this insertion. But it doesn't *require* it, and there's simply no reason to make this assumption. If we refrain from reading into the text the assumption that Jesus believed there was a divine reason for everything, the text is perfectly intelligible without the assertion. If we stick with the original Greek, we find it is more likely that Jesus was *negating* the question, not answering it—just as we saw him do in Luke 13.

On this reading, Jesus simply responded to the disciples' question by proclaiming, "Let God be glorified!" In effect Jesus was saying, "Who sinned, you ask? Wrong question! The only thing that matters is seeing the work of God revealed in this man." Jesus' whole ministry was about demonstrating "God's works" (Jn 9:3) and so he healed the man (Jn 9:6-8). Thus we see that in John 9 Jesus was not supporting the blueprint worldview. To the contrary, as in Luke 13, he was invalidating this worldview by rejecting the questions that arise from it.[16]

PHILOSOPHY AND THE BLUEPRINT WORLDVIEW

From the perspective of a theology centered on Jesus Christ the blueprint worldview is problematic. But it's also problematic on philosophical grounds. The blueprint worldview intensifies the problem of evil, and it is rooted in fundamental philosophical assumptions that are highly questionable.

The problem of evil. One of the chief problems in the Western philosophical tradition is reconciling the presence of evil with an all-good and all-powerful God. The problem, in a nutshell, is that if God is all-powerful, it seems he must have the ability to stop evil if he wants to. And if God is all-good, it seems he would want to. Yet evil persists.

The blueprint answer to this problem is that God is justified in ordaining or at least allowing evil to exist as a means of contributing to a greater good. In this view God could have created a world that was devoid of suffering, but he chose to include it because a creation with suffering is better in the long run than one without it. In the words of Augustine, God deemed it "more befitting His power and goodness to bring good out of evil than to prevent the evil from coming into existence."[17]

But it's very difficult to see how some of the more horrendous episodes of evil in this world contribute to a higher good. It's hard to believe that more good will come out of the pain and death of each Holocaust victim than if any one of them had been spared. It's hard to imagine how the unthinkable abuse of a helpless little boy contributes more to the overall good of creation than his safety. It's difficult to accept that each death in the World Trade Center and Pentagon attacks, and every broken heart that resulted from these attacks, somehow contributes to a "higher harmony." And it's difficult to accept that people in hell somehow contribute to the overall good of creation.

While blueprint theologians offer sophisticated responses in an attempt to avoid this conclusion, their position seems to implicate God in the very evil it attempts to explain. If God deemed the suffering of the Holocaust worth the good that would result from it, how is his thinking any different than the Nazis'? If every evil event could have been avoided had God so willed, how are we to avoid thinking of God as a conspirator in evil?

Not surprisingly, many who equate belief in God with this blueprint understanding of evil have abandoned belief altogether. Like Ivan in Dostoyevsky's *The Brothers Karamazov*, these people abandon belief in God on moral grounds. "I renounce the higher harmony altogether," Ivan announces. "It's not worth the tears of . . . one tortured child."[18] Any design that explicitly and specifically permits an innocent child to be tortured for a "greater purpose" is intrinsically immoral, he argues, and we are obliged to renounce it.

Believing as though it happened to you. Many who embrace the blueprint worldview don't seriously question it—until tragedy strikes home. It is easier to accept that everything is part of a marvelous divine plan when we are relatively insolated from the nightmarish aspects of life. But when *our* child is choked in childbirth, when *our* toddler is kidnapped or when *our* spouse is killed by terrorists, the divine plan does not seem so marvelous. Some who suffer such fates heroically press on, even finding comfort in the thought that their tragedy is somehow for the best. But many others are tormented by the thought. Some, such as Melanie, trudge on with a lifeless, passionless, empty relationship with God. Others end up revolting against God—or at least against their conception of God.

On one level it's understandable that we usually don't feel the full force of the nightmarish side of life until it hits home. After all, we all want to be happy. We are instinctively inclined to block out grotesque realities that disturb us. On another level, however, it is a frank testimony to our lack of thought and love: we don't allow the suffering of others to penetrate our minds and hearts. Only after a personal tragedy do we come to grips with the problem, because it is *our* personal problem—as though what happened to other humans was not our problem.

To live thoughtfully with Christlike love we must allow ourselves to be disturbed by the grotesque realities surrounding us and sympathetically enter into the nightmarish suffering of others. Tragedy strikes people every day. Children die in childbirth every day. Terrorists or other murderers steal the lives of spouses every day. Children are kidnapped, raped, sold into forced labor and killed every day. Over forty thousand people die of starvation and related diseases every day. Fully awake and fully loving human beings must not hear these things as abstract statistics, but empathetically enter into the experience of this ongoing nightmare. We must live with the empathetic awareness that there are, right now, loving parents who don't know where their children are or what's being done to them.

Our faith in God, our worldview, must be fully integrated with these experiences *as though they were our own*. As far as possible we must reconcile our faith in God with our own child dying in childbirth, our own spouse being killed by terrorists and our own family starving to death. Our brothers and sisters are experiencing these very nightmares even as you're reading this sentence! When we live, love and think in this fashion, I submit, the blueprint explanation for evil becomes much more difficult to accept.

The philosophical mistakes of the blueprint worldview. The final problem with the blueprint worldview is that it is based on faulty reasoning.

First, the belief that God is all-powerful does not mean that God *exercises* all power. It only means that God is the ultimate *source* of all power. Fallen people may value the ability to control others and thus project this attribute onto God (Mt 20:25-28). But the cross breaks all of our fallen assumptions about what God must be like. The cross reveals—and the rest of Scripture teaches (see chapter three)—that God empowers others to act on their own, against his own wishes if they so choose. The cross reveals that God is so sovereign he doesn't need to ensure he will always get his own way. There is, therefore, no reason to follow Augustine and others in maintaining that "the will of the omnipotent is always undefeated," if this is taken to mean that each event in history reveals God's omnipotent will. Earthly lords may aspire to an all-controlling form of lordship, but not the King of all kings and the Lord of all Lords (1 Tim 6:15; Rev 17:14; see also Mk 10:42-45).

Second, there is no reason to accept the conclusion of certain Hellenistic philosophers, repeated in much of the church's theological tradition, that a perfect being must be absolutely unchanging and impervious to outside influences. True, God is unchanging in terms of his perfect character (e.g. Mal 3:6; Heb 1:13; Jas 1:17). But as the incarnation and crucifixion reveal, because God's loving character is perfect, he can and does change in response to changing situations. Plato and many following him mistakenly thought that something can change only for the better or the worse. But in point of fact, people can change simply as an expression of who they are. Indeed, if their character is virtuous, they must be willing and able to change.

Possessing the ability to change is not a defect but a virtue. The inability to change is a defect. To illustrate, if a joyful person with a compassionate character enters a room in which a friend is grieving, he or she will immediately respond to the friend by adjusting his or her demeanor. People change in their response to others precisely because they are unchanging in their compassionate character. We would consider them cold and calloused if they didn't. The change doesn't make them better or worse. It just expresses the virtuous, unchanging character they possess.

A god who was never affected by anything outside of himself could not be perfectly loving and compassionate. If we believe God is unchanging in his perfect love, we must believe he *perfectly changes* in response to the changing situations of the people he loves. This is precisely what the incarnation and cross reveal about God. God is as perfect in his ability and willingness to change as he is in his unchanging character.

Similarly, there is no reason to conclude that a perfect being wouldn't experience a "before" and "after." There is nothing innately virtuous about being locked into an "eternal now." To the contrary, it's difficult to conceive of the personal, interacting, responsive God we find in the Bible limited in this fashion. And certainly, if all our thinking about God revolves around the person of Jesus Christ, the last thing we'd conclude about God is that he exists in an unchanging "eternal now." Jesus Christ is *God with us*, a human in time who responds to our desperate fallen condition. As such, he incarnates God's beautiful responsiveness and changeability we see throughout Scripture.[19]

CONCLUSION

The blueprint worldview is pervasive in church tradition and influences the thinking of many Christians and non-Christians. Though many people find comfort in the blueprint, it has wounded many others, such as Melanie. The blueprint worldview also has contributed to passivity in the church. In contrast to the ministry of Jesus, the church, at least to some extent, has been conditioned to accept calamity and suffering as coming from the Father's hand when they really come from Satan. This has tarnished the character of God. Common sense has difficulty affirming God as the ultimate explanation for every event in history while denying he is morally responsible for those events. Consequently, many people have rejected Christianity or belief in God.

Against this perspective, I have argued that the blueprint worldview is not based on sound philosophical reasoning and, even more importantly, is not consistent with the picture of God we get from Jesus Christ.

If our picture of God is singularly focused on Christ, as it ought to be, we must see God as fighting evil, not willing it.

Merely affirming this much, however, does not address how to interpret suffering and evil in the light of Christ. If events don't necessarily happen because God ordains or specifically allows them, why do they happen? Does denying a specific divine reason for every specific event mean that God is not all-powerful? What are we to make of Bible passages that depict God as orchestrating suffering and evil? Don't these support the blueprint worldview? These questions and others like them will be addressed in the remaining chapters of this book.

THREE

FREEDOM AND RISK

The most significant difficulty with the blueprint worldview is that it presupposes a picture of God and his relationship to the world that is at odds with the picture revealed in Jesus Christ. Jesus didn't come to declare that everything already manifests the Father's will. He came, rather, to *establish* the Father's will, because the world as it now is *doesn't* consistently manifest God's will. Jesus came to confront and eventually overthrow everything that does not line up with his Father's plan for creation. Far from revealing a blueprint worldview in which God's will is always carried out, Jesus' ministry reveals a warfare worldview in which God wars against those that oppose him.

Of course, Christ's resurrection also reveals that God has conquered evil in principle and thus God's overall plan for creation will ultimately be accomplished. The kingdom of darkness has been dealt a decisive deathblow, and it is now just a matter of time before it is utterly vanquished. But this truth doesn't negate the claim that to some extent human and spiritual agents can continue to thwart God's will. To the contrary, the ongoing reality of the warfare God engages in presupposes that they can.

How are we to make sense of this fact? How could the omnipotent God's creation become a war zone in which he has to genuinely fight to establish his will? Indeed, how could he create a world in which he, the omnipotent God, ends up suffering at the hands of his creation and experiencing a godforsaken death on the cross?

To answer this question, I will first reconsider the purpose for which God created the world and argue that achieving this purpose requires that humans and angels possess free will. I then show that Scripture confirms human and angelic freedom and that this is how God's creation became the war zone that it presently is. I conclude by showing how this view affects our understanding of the church's mission, highlighting the harm done by the appropriation of the blueprint worldview.

GOD'S GOAL REQUIRES RISK

The purpose is love. The most basic and yet most profound teaching of the Bible is that "God is love" (1 Jn 4:8, 16). He is revealed to be a God who is triune—Father, Son and Holy Spirit (see Mt 3:16; 28:19; Jn 14:26; 15:26)—who's very essence is an eternal, loving relationship. He created the world out of love and for the purpose of expanding his love.

We find this beautiful goal succinctly expressed in Jesus' prayer in John 17. On behalf of his disciples and all who would believe their word, Jesus asked:

> As you, Father, are in me and I am in you, may they also be in us, so that the world may believe that you have sent me. The glory that you have given me I have given them, so that they may be one, as we are one, I in them and you in me, that they may become completely one, so that the world may know that you have sent me and have loved them even as you have loved me. . . . I made your name known to them, and I will make it known, so that the love with which you have loved me may be in them, and I in them." (Jn 17:21-23, 26)

In this prayer we learn that God the Father desires that we dwell in Christ and Christ in us, just as Christ dwells in the Father and he in Christ. Indeed, the Father wants us to participate in and reflect the loving union that he has with Christ. The goal, in other words, is for the perfect triune love of God to be *manifested to* people, *replicated in* people and *reflected back from* people. This is why God created the world. The whole of creation is meant to express and embody the eternal triune love that God is. It exists to glorify God.

Humans are to glorify God by expressing his love and authority as we rule the earth. God wants to be Lord over all creation, but because he is the triune God of love, he doesn't want to do this unilaterally. Of course he could have created a world where we *have* to do his will, but it would have been a creation devoid of love. Instead, God wants to rule creation through coregents, free agents who through love apply his sovereign will to the earth. God therefore created us "in his image" that *we* might "have dominion" and "subdue" the earth (Gen 1:26-28). As we receive, embody and reflect his love, we are to do in a little way what God does in a big way, namely, rule over the portion of the cosmos he has given us.

The risk of love. Knowing the goal of creation helps us understand how creation became a war zone. God created the world out of love and for the purpose of love. But as all emotionally healthy people intuitively know, love must be chosen. And choice means that a person can say no. Unless people can choose not to love, they can't genuinely choose to love. The possibility of the one is built into the possibility of the other. Love simply cannot be coerced or programmed into people.

Up to the time of Augustine the church understood and emphasized this point. The church fathers repeatedly stressed that love and virtue require morally responsible choice. Thus they taught that God's mode of operation in running the world is not coercion but persuasion.[1] A creation in which love is the goal must incorporate risk. Creation doesn't have to have *actual* evil, but it must allow for the *possibility* of evil—if the possibility of genuine love is to exist.

This is why God commanded humans to have dominion over the world (Gen 1:26-28). If we weren't free to disobey God, a command would be unnecessary; we would do what God created us to do automatically. Because God wants his will carried out in love, he empowers humans to carry out his command freely. And this, of course, means we can refuse to carry out his command if we choose.

God gave Adam and Eve free will in the Garden. The purpose of this freedom was that they might choose to remain in loving union with God. But because it was a union of *love*, it had to be possible for Adam and Eve to reject it. The possibility of rejection is expressed by the forbidden fruit of "tree of the knowledge of good and evil" (Gen 2:17). This represents the frightful possibility of choosing to rebel against God and defining "good and evil" for ourselves. Tragically, the first couple chose to disobey God, thereby bringing judgment on themselves and their descendants (Gen 3:1-19). This disobedience was not part of God's original plan; it was a rejection of God's plan. Yet the possibility of this rejection had to exist if God's original plan was to be possible. His plan is for people to administrate his creation as they receive, replicate and reflect back God's triune love.

THE BIBLE AND HUMAN OPPOSITION

God's plea to follow him. The Bible repeatedly confirms that people are created with a measure of freedom. We find God giving people choices throughout the Bible. For example, God tells the Israelites in the Old Testament:

> See, I set before you today life and prosperity, death and destruction. For I command you today to love the LORD your God, to walk in his ways . . . then you will live and increase, and the LORD your God will bless you in the land you are entering to possess.
>
> But if your heart turns away and you are not obedient, and if you are drawn away to bow down to other gods and worship them, I declare to you this day that you will certainly be destroyed. . . .
>
> I have set before you life and death, blessings and curses. Now choose life, so that you and your children may live. (Deut 30:15-19 NIV)

God gives Israel the choice to choose life, which is loving him, or to choose death, which is rejecting him. God obviously longs for his people to choose life, but ultimately it is *up to them* to decide. They are, in this respect, free.

Another example of the Lord placing choices before people, calling on them to choose to follow him, is found in Ezekiel 18.

> If a man is righteous and does what is lawful and right . . . he shall surely live, says the Lord GOD. . . .
>
> The person who sins shall die. . . .
>
> But if the wicked turn away from all their sins . . . they shall surely live; they shall not die. . . . Have I any pleasure in the death of the wicked, says the Lord GOD, and not rather that they should turn from their ways and live? . . .
>
> Cast away from you all the transgressions that you have committed against me, and get yourselves a new heart and a new spirit! Why will you die, O house of Israel? For I have no pleasure in the death of anyone, says the Lord GOD. Turn, then, and live. (Ezek 18:5, 9, 20-21, 23, 31-32)

The Lord gives individuals the choice of embracing his ways or not. If they choose to follow him, they live. If not, they die. The Lord emphatically expresses his will in this passage: *he doesn't want anyone to perish.* He takes no pleasure in the death of the wicked. Rather, he wants everyone to embrace the life he offers. But God created people free because he wants them to follow him from their own heart, not from a prescribed blueprint. This means that with regard to any individual God may not get his way.

The center that originates action. The Bible depicts people as the free originators of their own actions and thus as morally responsible for these actions. For example, Jesus taught, "The good person out of the good treasure *of the heart* produces good, and the evil person out of evil treasure produces evil; for it is out of the abundance *of the heart* that the mouth speaks" (Lk 6:45, italics added). Similarly, Jesus taught that it was out of a person's heart that "evil intentions, murder, adultery, fornication, theft, false witness, [and] slander" arise (Mt 15:19). These are not things that God desires or intentionally plans for his creation. They originate in a person's own heart.

The Bible uniformly depicts evil intentions and actions in this way. To give just a few illustrations, King Solomon is said to have done "what was evil in the sight of the LORD . . . . [B]ecause his heart had turned away from the LORD, the God of Israel" (1 Kings 11:6, 9). So too King Rehoboam "did evil, for he did not set his heart to seek the LORD" (2 Chron 12:14). Similarly, Zedekiah "did what was evil in the sight of the LORD" because "[h]e stiffened his neck and hardened his heart against turning to the LORD, the God of Israel" (2 Chron 36:12-13). And the reason why Jerusalem had degenerated to such a low moral point during the time of Jeremiah, according to the Bible, was because God's people had "a stubborn and rebellious heart" and had "turned aside and gone away" (Jer 5:23). The Lord had been calling on them to "wash your heart clean of wickedness so that you may be saved." And he had asked them, "How long shall your evil schemes lodge within you?" (Jer 4:14). But the people obstinately refused. In all these instances we see that evil originates not in God's plan but in "the heart" of people resisting his plan. As Jeremiah says, the evil is lodged within us. Ultimately, we are the final explanation of our own behavior.

The pain of God's heart. The Bible also asserts that evil originates with free agents by revealing that God is frequently frustrated by the way people obstinately resist his loving plans (e.g., Is 63:10; Acts 7:51; Heb 3:8, 15; 4:7; cf. Eph 4:30). Indeed, God's heart breaks over people's rebelliousness (e.g., Ex 33:3, 5; 34:9; Deut 9:6, 13; 10:16; 31:27; Judg 2:19; 2 Kings 17:14; 2 Chron 30:8; 36:13; Neh 9:16; Is 46:12; 48:4; Jer 7:26; Hos 4:16). Jesus' lament over Jerusalem clearly reveals how human rebellion pains God's heart:

Jerusalem, Jerusalem, the city that kills the prophets and stones those who are sent to it! How often have I desired to gather your children together as a hen gathers her brood under her wings, and you were not willing! (Mt 23:37)

Christ, who is our picture of God, earnestly longs for everyone in the city of Jerusalem to come to him and receive the life he has to offer. But even though he was the Son of God, their response was not up to him: it was up to them. In a creation populated with free agents, God doesn't always get what he wants. Augustine and the church tradition that followed him were simply mistaken when they insisted that "the will of the omnipotent is always undefeated." Because God desires a creation in which love is a reality, he allows his will to be defeated to some extent.

Rejecting the plan of God. The Bible explicitly states that people can and do thwart God's will. The lawyers and Sadducees of Jesus' day "rejected God's purpose for themselves" (Lk 7:30) by refusing the ministry of John the Baptist. Isaiah's message to the children of Israel is even more explicit:

Oh, rebellious children, says the LORD,
who carry out a plan, but not mine;
who make an alliance, but against my will,
    adding sin to sin. (Is 30:1)

Because they were free agents, the Israelites had the power to accept or reject God's will. Their rebellion was not part of a divine blueprint. They were not *fulfilling* God's sovereign will by rebelling against him. They were rebelling precisely because they were *rejecting* God's sovereign will.

God's frustration, regret and disappointment. Examples of God's frustration and disappointment over the choices humans make—or refuse to make—permeate the Bible. To give just a few examples, the sorrow and frustration in the words of the Lord are palpable in Ezekiel: "I sought for anyone among them who would repair the wall and stand in the breach before me on behalf of the land, so that I would not destroy it," the Lord decries. But unfortunately, he concludes, "I found no one. Therefore I have poured out my indignation upon them" (Ezek 22:30-31). This passage is a remarkable testimony to the urgency of prayer, but also to the importance of freedom in general.[2] If anyone would have heeded the Lord's earnest attempt to raise up an intercessor, the disaster that befell Israel would have been avoided.

The passage clearly presupposes that it was not the Lord's will to punish Israel. Indeed, bringing judgment on nations is never God's ideal will. He may will it as the lesser of two evils; but it is not part of his original will for creation. To the contrary, it is always his sad response to people resolving their will against his.

In Jeremiah the Lord tells us that whenever he prophesies about the future destruction of a nation, it is in hope that the nation will repent of their wicked ways so he might "change [his] mind about the disaster that [he] intended to bring on it" (Jer 18:8). The Lord is willing to adjust his plans when people adjust their ways, for God has no delight in the destruction of the wicked (Ezek 18:23, 32; 33:11; 2 Pet 3:9). The Lord "does not willingly afflict or grieve anyone" (Lam 3:33).

The same sentiment is expressed in passages describing God's sorrow at the way things have turned out because of human decisions. For example, because of the depravity prior to the flood "the LORD was sorry that he made humankind on the earth, and it grieved him to his heart" (Gen. 6:6). If the will of the omnipotent can never be defeated, then he must have willed human depravity prior to the flood. But in this case it becomes impossible to explain why a holy God would will such an evil thing and then genuinely regret the way his creation turned out.

God experienced a similar frustration over Saul. Though God reluctantly gave in to the Israelite request for a king, God nevertheless intended to bless King Saul and his household for many generations (1 Sam 13:13). But Saul's heart turned from God, and the Lord told Samuel, "I regret that I made Saul king, for he has turned back from following me" (1 Sam 15:11; see also v. 35). God changed his mind about Saul and removed him from his office. But this was not God's ideal will. He did it as a necessary and just response to Saul's own free decisions.

Many times the Lord expresses disappointment and even surprise at the stubbornness of his people. Through Jeremiah, for example, the Lord says about Israel, "I thought, 'After she has done all this she will return to me'; but she did not return" (Jer 3:7). And again, several verses later, he says:

> I thought
>> how I would set you among my children. . . .
> And I thought you would call me, My Father,
>> and would not turn from following me.
> Instead, as a faithless wife . . .
>> you have been faithless to me. (Jer 3:19-20)

It seems clear that if God can hope for one outcome only to be disappointed by another, it must be possible for humans to thwart his will in some instances (see Is 5:1-5).

Finally, nowhere is our ability to freely stymie God's purpose more evident than in the damnation of people. The Bible teaches that God desires that every person accept his love and be saved (e.g., 1 Tim 2:4, 4:10; 2 Pet 3:9; cf. Ezek 18:23, 32; 33:11). There is no partiality in God that leads him to love one person more than another or to arbitrarily select some for salvation rather than others (Deut 10:17; 2 Chron 19:7; Acts 10:34; Rom 2:11; Jas 3:17). God wants *all* to be saved, and he created them with the hope that they would be saved.

Yet the Bible also makes it clear that many people refuse God's salvation. Even though Jesus died "for the sins of the whole world" (1 Jn 2:2), and even though God is always working in people's hearts to influence them to accept him, some people love darkness rather than light (Jn 3:19). Because people must be free for love to be genuine, they have the capacity to thwart God's will and bring destruction on themselves.

When people refuse God's plan for their lives, it's not because their destruction fits into God's mysterious blueprint for creation. To the contrary, throughout their lives God works to save them—which is why he is frustrated with their abstinence. "All day long," the Lord says, "I have held out my hands to a disobedient and contrary people" (Rom 10:21). God truly grieves when the people he loves choose to resist him.

The point of these observations is that people do have free will. They originate their own actions. Hence, they are the final explanation for what they choose to do. When people decide to cause suffering and act in other evil ways, it makes sense to ask why *they* made the decision. But it's not reasonable or necessary to wonder why *God* had them make the decision. Free agents make their own decisions. Free agents devise their own plans. And the decisions and plans of these free agents do not necessarily express God's decisions and plans.

God's plan has always been that we would align our will with his will. But because his plan is a plan of love, this alignment could not be preprogrammed or coerced. The possibility of rejecting it had to exist. If love is the end, freedom must be the means to that end.

THE BIBLE AND ANGELIC OPPOSITION

Angelic freedom. Acknowledging that humans have free will explains much, but not all, of the evil in the world. To fully account for the wartorn nature of this creation we need to understand that God created angels as free agents as well.

The Bible provides us with few details about God's dealings with angels, but we are told that certain angels rebelled against God in the past and continue to resist his will in the present (2 Pet 2:4; Jude 1:6; Rev 12:7-9; see also Mt 25:41; Jn 8:44; Eph 6:12). This alone is enough to prove that angels are free, for it's impossible for an angel to reject the desires of its Creator if it lacked the capacity to choose.

The Bible teaches us that the head of the angelic rebellion is a very powerful being named Satan, meaning "the adversary." The scope of Satan's power is reflected by Jesus calling him "the ruler of this world" (Jn 12:31; 14:30; 16:11). The term *ruler* was used in ancient secular contexts to denote the highest official in a city or region.[3] Therefore, Jesus acknowledged that Satan is the highest power of this fallen world, at least in terms of his present influence.

When Satan tempted Jesus by offering him all "authority" over "all the kingdoms of this world," Jesus did not dispute Satan's claim that this was his to offer (Lk 4:5-6). Jesus simply refused to give in to the demand that he worship Satan in order to get these kingdoms. Consistent with this, other passages in the Bible teach that the whole world is "under the power of the evil one" (1 Jn 5:19), that Satan is "the god of this world" (2 Cor 4:4) and "the ruler of the power of the air" (Eph 2:2). The explanation for why God's creation looks like a war zone is because, according to the Bible, it *is* a war zone! Far from following a meticulous divine blueprint, creation is now governed by a powerful being who resists God's purposes at every turn.

The Bible depicts this evil ruler as the leader of a unified and pervasive army of spiritual powers. Satan is thus called "the ruler of demons" (Mt 9:34), and fallen angels are called "his angels" (Mt 25:41). Jesus and other New Testament authors assumed that these fallen spirits influence what transpires in our world. Many forms of physical oppression were diagnosed by Jesus and his disciples as being directly or indirectly influenced by evil spirits. Blindness, deafness, muteness and deformities are not always mere physical ailments. They are evidence of our being under a spiritual regime at odds with God's purposes. So too spiritual blindness (2 Cor 4:4), hindrances in ministry and evangelism (1 Thess 2:18), delays in prayer (Dan 10:1-13), the behavior of evil people (Jn 13:2), temptation and discouragement (1 Tim 3:7; 2 Tim 2:25-26), the struggle with "strongholds" (2 Cor 10:3-5), false and legalistic religious teachings (1 Tim 4:1-4), persecutions (Rev 2:10), some life-threatening "natural" phenomenon (Mk 4:39), and even death (Heb 2:14) are attributed to the influence of the devil or other rebel spirits.[4]

Warfare and the ministry of Jesus. Jesus came to end this "enemy oc-cupation" of the earth. To bring this enemy occupation to an end and take back the property of this "kingdom," someone must first tie up "the strong man" who oversees the whole operation (Mk 3:27). This could only be done when "one stronger than [the strong man] attacks him and overpowers him" and thus "takes away his armor in which he trusted" (Lk 11:22). This was what Jesus understood himself to be doing through his teaching, healing, exorcisms and especially his death and resurrec-tion. His whole ministry was about overpowering the "fully armed" strong man who guarded his property (Lk 11:21)—the earth and its in-habitants who rightfully belong to God. Jesus tied up the strong man so that he (and later, his church) could pillage the strong man's kingdom. He came to "destroy the works of the devil" (1 Jn 3:8; see also Heb 2:14), disarm the principalities and powers (Col 2:14-15), put all God's ene-mies under his feet (Eph 1:22; Heb 1:13), and thus establish the earth as God's kingdom. In short, he came to set the world free from the oppres-sion of its evil ruler.

THE CHURCH AND WARFARE

The growing mustard seed. Jesus taught that the kingdom of God is like a mustard seed. It's among the smallest of all seeds when planted, but it eventually grows to become the largest shrub in the garden (Mt 13:31-32). The point is that though Jesus defeated Satan in principle and reestab-lished the kingdom of God on the earth, the earth doesn't automatically revert back to the way God intended it to be. Through Jesus' death and resurrection, the seed has been planted, but it needs to grow. The "strong man" has been tied up, and now God's troops need to "pillage the house."

God could do all this himself, of course. But because God is a social being and his goal is love, he chooses to work through mediators (hu-mans and angels) who lovingly choose to cooperate with his plans. How they use their freedom genuinely affects the extent to which God's will is done "on earth as it is in heaven."

The church is the corporate expression of all those who have said yes to God's saving grace and are responding to his call to mediate his will on earth. As such the church is initiating God's goal for humans to recover their rightful place as his coregents, who "subdue" and "have dominion" over the earth. Our original parents surrendered this authority to Satan, but now through Jesus, God is giving it back to us.

Storming the gates of hell. Jesus' first teaching about the church in the Gospels is that "the gates of Hades [hell] will not prevail against it" (Mt 16:18). Jesus is saying that God wants those who follow him—the church—to expand the kingdom of God, and his promise is that the kingdom of Satan will not be able to withstand this expansion. Jesus empowers all who believe in him to once again have dominion over the earth by vanquishing all forces that oppose God's will.

In God's plan, therefore, the church is the vehicle for finishing off the work Jesus began. Christians can't do this on their own, of course. Jesus himself is present in and with them to accomplish this task. This is why the church is called "the body of Christ" (Rom 12:4-5; 1 Cor 12:12-27; Eph 1:22-23; 4:4; 5:23). But this doesn't negate the fact that those who follow Christ have important choices to make in how they live. As it was in the beginning, God wants to rule through mediators who freely choose to cooperate with him by applying his will on the earth. God's will is that through his disciples—the church—he confronts "the gates of Hades" and takes back from his arch enemy what rightfully belongs to him and the people he has authorized to rule.

The "gates of Hades" represents everything that resists God's loving will for the earth. Whenever people believe lies, the church is to storm the gates of Hades by proclaiming truth. Whenever people are treated as worthless, the church is to break through the gates of Hades, proclaiming that God created all people to have infinite value. Whenever people are oppressed by poverty, the church is to proclaim and work for justice. Whenever people are physically afflicted, the church is to proclaim and practice healing. Whenever people are oppressed by demonic powers, the church is to proclaim and practice deliverance. Whenever people are separated by racism, the church is to work to manifest the one new humanity Jesus died to create (Eph 2:14). All these evils constitute the "gates of Hades" the church must overthrow. By word and especially by deed, we are to express the truth that God is unsurpassable love, which he wants all to participate in.

The heartbeat of the church is reflected in the way Jesus taught us to pray. We are to pray that the Father's will be done "on earth as it is in heaven" (Mt 6:10). This prayer, and all the activity Christians are involved in, presupposes that the Father's will is *not* yet being done on earth as it is in heaven. God's heavenly will is being resisted by spiritual forces and by people who don't want it accomplished on earth. The church is to expand the kingdom—to grow the mustard seed—by speaking and living the truth in love.

THE HARM OF THE BLUEPRINT WORLDVIEW

Resignation versus revolt. Herein lies one of the greatest tragedies of the blueprint worldview. When people believe that everything is *already* part of God's "secret plan," they won't work with passion and urgency *to establish* God's will on earth as it is in heaven. Rather, as much popular Christian piety reveals, they resign themselves to all that happens as coming "from a Father's hand." They pray for the ability to accept things more than the ability to change things. They seek the power to comfort more than the power to deliver. This quasi-peaceful resignation expresses the kind of piety sought throughout history by pagans—ancient Stoics, practitioners of most Eastern religions and adherents of all forms of religious fatalism. But it definitely is not the kind of piety Jesus encouraged us to seek.

Jesus taught a *piety of revolt*, not resignation. To be sure, Jesus' people are empowered by the Spirit to have a peace that surpasses all understanding, and to experience and dispense comfort in supernatural ways (Phil 4:7). We are able—even commanded—to trust God with every aspect of our lives and therefore to be free from all anxiety (Mt 6:25-34). But this peace is not because we believe that everything is unfolding according to God's plan. It is a far greater peace than that.

The peace that God gives can be experienced in the midst of events that are not part of God's plan. It's an abiding tranquillity we experience even while resisting and revolting against circumstances contrary to God's plan. It's joy that does not waver even though we live in an environment where Satan is god. It's the peace of knowing that though creation is ripped by cosmic war, God will be victorious over evil in the end. Then all who follow Christ will reign with him (2 Tim 2:12; Rev 20:6; 22:5), and the battle will have been worth it (Rom 8:18). Divine serenity comes from knowing that nothing can separate us from the love of Christ—and in the end that is all that matters (Rom 8:31-39). The peace that God gives is far superior to the "peace" that believes all events are unfolding according to an inflexible divine plan.

When we trade our mandate to revolt against Satan for an attitude of resignation, we end up accepting things that come from Satan as coming from the hand of God! We trade in a perfect peace (that motivates us to fight) for a worldly peace (that leads to passivity). We tarnish the character of God by confusing his activity with Satan's, and we undermine the mission of the church. We trade the legitimate challenge to overcome actual evil for the illegitimate challenge of accepting that God's will is ultimately behind every evil event.

When we understand that God created free human and angelic beings, we no longer struggle with an unsolvable intellectual problem, and we are motivated to confront rather than accept the evils in the world. If it's true that "the whole world lies under the power of the evil one" (1 Jn 5:19), we shouldn't be surprised that the world is full of evil. But if it's also true that Jesus has defeated this enemy and has made us "his body," then there are things we can and must do about the evil in the world.

CONCLUSION

How has this world, created by an all-powerful God, become a war zone? How is it possible that this all-powerful God was crucified by his creation? And how does his godforsaken death put an end to this war? So long as we think of God's greatness in terms of sheer power, there is no adequate answer to these questions. But when we turn to the cross itself and read Scripture in the light of this cross, the answer is apparent.

God's greatness is most fundamentally about love. God created the world out of love and for the purpose of love. And this requires that he created free agents. There can be no love without risk. The possibility of war, therefore, is built into the possibility of love.

When we keep our eyes fixed on Christ as God's definitive self-revelation, we discover that every aspect of creation not in sync with the beauty of God revealed on the cross is the result of war, not part of a divine blueprint. Whatever does not reflect the unsurpassable love and beauty we see in Christ may be assumed to be the result of choices that are not in line with God's will. In the light of the cross we may conclude that the world looks like a war zone because it is a war zone. But in light of the resurrection we know that the way the world looks now is not the way it will look in the future. God's will shall be done "on earth as it is in heaven."

We who align ourselves with God's will—the church—are to receive God's love and replicate that love in the world around us. But even here there is freedom, and therefore there is risk on God's part. We are God's partners, not God's robots. We have made the decisive choice to accept God's love, receive God's forgiveness and acknowledge Christ as Lord of our life. But our choices in life still make a difference. God has given us real say-so to help bring about the future God desires. Thus Scripture calls us coworkers with God (1 Cor 3:9; 2 Cor 6:1; see also 1 Thess 3:2).

The mustard seed has been planted, and the outcome of the war is ensured. Its growth and effect on specific people and in specific areas of life depend in large part on the fidelity of the church in carrying out its mission. Yet there are many battles to be fought between D-day (the cross and resurrection) and V-day (Christ's return). Hence, there are many questions Jesus' disciples must answer daily: Will we live the kingdom life God calls us to live? Will we pray as God calls us to pray? Will we love as God calls us to love? Will we die to ourselves and live in Christ, or will we give in to the self-centered materialism of our culture?

Our choices matter. Much hangs in the balance. Our freedom is God's risk and our dignity.

FOUR

COMPLEXITY AND WAR

God made humans and angels free and empowered them to affect himself and influence what comes to pass. This explains how this world created by the all-good God became a war zone. If love is the goal, the possibility of war must be its price. But this answer doesn't explain why any *particular* instance of evil occurs. It doesn't explain the arbitrary way blessings and curses seem to be distributed. And it doesn't answer the age-old question, What did I do to deserve this?

WHERE TO LOCATE THE MYSTERY

Why is one infant born sickly and deformed when at the same time another is born perfectly healthy? Why does tragedy repeatedly strike one family while another seems to enjoy uninterrupted peace? Why does a godly, caring woman like Melanie have her "miraculously" conceived child choked to death during childbirth when other, uncaring women have healthy babies? Why, in short, is the world so arbitrary and unfair?

This apparent arbitrariness carries over to the way God answers prayer. While most people who regularly pray tell of occasions when their prayers were miraculously answered, they also admit that there is no rhyme or reason as to why some prayers are answered and others aren't. A quickly spoken prayer to heal a sprained ankle seems to work, while a multitude of persistent, fervent prayers for terminal cancer have no discernible effect. A wealthy couple testifies how God helped them find "the house of their dreams," while another person's desperate prayer for food to keep her children from starvation is unheeded. One person praises God for sparing his life by miraculously delaying his arrival at the World Trade Center, while hundreds of others wonder why their prayers to protect their loved ones that morning seemed to be ignored. Melanie's prayer to have a child seemed to be miraculously answered, but her prayer for a safe delivery seemed to be ignored.

Appealing to the free will of humans and angels explains why evil *in general* must be allowed. But it doesn't explain why any *particular* evil occurs. And it doesn't explain God's seemingly arbitrary involvement in the world. Why does God intervene to stop evil in one instance but not in another?

I dare to offer something of an explanation to this question. But I must confess at the start that what I'm actually attempting to explain is *why there can be no final explanation to this question.* The arbitrariness of life is a mystery. Yet everything hangs on where we locate this arbitrariness and mystery. Everything hangs on what we think we can and can't know.

We customarily assume we know a lot about creation but very little about God. After all, we can see creation, but we can't see God. Creation is finite, but God is infinite. While we can explore creation, we can't explore God. And since it's usually assumed that God directly or indirectly controls everything that occurs in creation, we are inclined to attribute the arbitrariness of creation to his mysterious will.

In this chapter I argue for the opposite view. Because of God's self-revelation in Jesus Christ, we can be confident of our knowledge about God's character and general purposes for our life. What we can hardly begin to fathom, however, is *the vast complexity of creation,* a creation that includes an untold number of human and spiritual free agents whose decisions affect much that comes to pass.

This is not at all to suggest that we know everything about God. To the contrary, there are aspects of God that are utterly beyond comprehension. But we can know what is most important to know, namely, that *when we see Jesus Christ we see God.* In Christ we confidently know God's character and purposes. Hence, unless we have good reason to think otherwise, we can assume that whatever appears inconsistent with the character and purposes of God revealed in Jesus Christ ultimately comes from agents who oppose God. However, we know next to nothing about how these agents' wills affect what comes to pass.

Behind every particular event in history lies an impenetrably vast matrix of interlocking free decisions made by humans and angels. We experience life as largely arbitrary because we can't fathom the causal chains that lie behind every particular event. In Christ, God's character and purposes are not mysterious, but the vast complexity of causal chains is. The mystery of evil, therefore, is about an unfathomably complex and war-torn creation, not about God's character and purposes in creation.

To defend this thesis I will first critique the blueprint approach to explaining the arbitrariness of life. Then I discuss Job, a book of the Bible that addresses this very topic. I believe that in contrast to the blueprint explanation of life's arbitrariness, Job locates the mystery of evil in the complexity and war-torn nature of the cosmos, not in the unfathomable will of the Creator.

DIVINE PUNISHMENT AND THE ARBITRARINESS
OF SUFFERING

Punishment and the explanation of suffering. In the Christian tradition since Augustine, the most common explanation for the apparent arbitrariness of life and God's interaction with humanity has been God's mysterious will—his "secret plan," as Calvin says. Whether or not a child is born healthy is ultimately decided by God. If we ask why God brings misfortune on certain people, the most common answer is that he is using the misfortune to punish or discipline them (see chapter two).

I concede the explanation that suffering happens as punishment or discipline is found in both the Old and New Testaments (e.g., Heb 12:4-11). But there are several important points about this biblical motif that qualify it as a general explanation for why people suffer.

First, nowhere is this explanation of suffering put forth as a general explanation for the problem of evil in Scripture. Indeed, the only time an explicit connection is made between divine punishment and evil in general is to *deny* that such a connection can be made. For example, the psalmist repeatedly complains that suffering and blessing are meted out to the righteous and unrighteous arbitrarily. This is one of the central points of the book of Job.

This denial also occurs in the ministry of Jesus. When certain people assumed that those murdered by Pilate or killed by a collapsing tower were being punished by God, Jesus emphatically denied it (Lk 13:1-5). When his disciples inquired into whose sin was responsible for a man being born blind, Jesus invalidated the question and simply proclaimed, "Let God be glorified" (Jn 9:1-6).

Even more significantly, Jesus *never* suggests that any of the multitude of afflicted or demonized people he ministered to were being disciplined or punished. Rather, he suggests that such afflictions or demonizations were the direct or indirect result of Satan being the "ruler" of this world (e.g., Jn 12:31). Though every person Jesus ministered to was a sinner, he uniformly treated them as casualties of war. He demonstrated the Father's will for these people by healing them and delivering them. If we believe that Christ is the one and only Word and image of God—the definitive revelation of who God is and of his purposes for us—our attitude toward all suffering, whether our own or that of others, must be in line with his.

Punishment and radical evil. Second, there is a world of difference between encouraging Christians facing persecution to see God refining their faith in the process (Heb 12:4-11) and encouraging a mother of a stillborn child to see this as God's way of teaching her a lesson. While we certainly must believe that God is always working to bring good *out of evil* (Rom 8:28), in most circumstances it is presumptuous to suggest that God specifically allows or brings about suffering *in order to* discipline a person. Apart from divine revelation, how could we possibly know this? But this presumption morphs to cruel absurdity when we are speaking of horrors like a man mourning his murdered wife or a mother grieving over her stillborn child.

This way of thinking takes the cruel arbitrariness of life and deifies it by projecting it onto God. When this is done, the beautiful clarity of God's loving will revealed in Christ and centered on the cross is obscured by a nonbiblical picture of a God of power. And Jesus' simple words "If you see me, you see the Father" are qualified by every terror-stricken scream of torture throughout history. For presumably we can see "the hand of a father" mysteriously behind these events as well!

If there is a lesson to be learned from people's experience of radical evil, it usually isn't apparent, especially to those experiencing it. Are we to believe that God punishes people in horrifying ways without telling them why? And what are we to make of Jesus explicitly telling us that tragedies do not happen for this reason? Towers fall and bloody massacres occur on the just and the unjust alike (Lk 13:1-5). Moreover, isn't one of the central messages of the cross that God himself has suffered for all sin (Jn 1:29; 1 Jn 2:2)? Why then should we suppose that God is still using tragedies to punish people?

Along these same lines, notice that almost all of the reward and punishment teaching of the Bible is given by God to Israel, not to humanity in general. God's plan was to teach this one nation how to walk faithfully as a covenant partner with him in order to reach the entire world. Israel was to be the yeast God mixed with the whole world "until all of it was leavened" (Mt 13:33). The blessings and curses Israel experienced were predicated on their covenantal fidelity to God and thus can't be assumed to reflect God's uniform treatment of all people at all times.

Frankly, if God is bringing about or allowing specific instances of suffering for teaching purposes, he isn't being very effective. Unlike Old Testament Israel, most people who suffer radical evil aren't informed by God why they're suffering. As happened with Melanie, they must guess at the reason behind the tragedy in their life.

Even more poignantly, the experience of radical evil crushes people at least as often as it builds them up. While Christians frequently testify how their tragedy was turned to a good purpose, there are just as many untold stories of people whose faith and character were devastated by tragedy. In this light the effectiveness of God's teaching program seems dubious at best.

A teaching technique that orchestrates one person's death to teach someone else a lesson is perplexing. In Melanie's case, for example, it's not clear why God would be more concerned with teaching her an undisclosed lesson than with protecting her baby's life. And it's certainly clear that the baby learned nothing from being choked to death. Again, it doesn't seem that God's teaching program is effective if this is indeed what he is up to.

God's love and justice. Third, even in the Old Testament when God is said to discipline individuals or nations with hardship, it is never presented as part of God's eternal plan. Instead, it's depicted as a necessary *response* to sinful choices people were making. This is God's "tough love." As we saw in the last chapter, it grieves God to do such things. He "does not willingly afflict or grieve anyone" (Lam 3:33), though in response to sin he sometimes has to.

Indeed, the Bible depicts God as struggling over whether or not he can bear to bring judgment on his covenantal people who deserve it.

How can I give you up, Ephraim?
    How can I hand you over, O Israel? . . .
My heart recoils within me;
    my compassion grows warm and tender. (Hos 11:8)

The passage depicts God's tender love and holy justice wrestling with one another (see also 1 Chron 21:14-15; Ezek 20:5-22).

Other passages reveal that God changed his mind after he had resolved to bring judgment on Israel, even though he had prophesied that he would do so (e.g., Jer 18:1-10; Jon 3:1-10). God is just, yet his love can hardly bear seeing the consequences of what his justice requires. As much as they deserve it, he takes no delight in punishing the wicked.

The conflict within God is resolved, as it were, on the cross of Calvary. God's mercy triumphs over judgment (Jas 2:13; see also Ps 30:5; Is 54:7). And this is why the cross decisively reveals God's heart and will toward all people. God loves sinners so much he himself decides to suffer the just wrath their sin deserves. He experiences what is antithetical to himself (sin and separation from God) so that those who have set themselves in antithesis to his will can be perfectly reconciled to him. The cross shows that God's unwavering heart toward people is to forgive them and have them participate in the unending ecstatic dance of his own loving triune fellowship.

As people who reflect on suffering in the light of the cross, and as people who know God as he has been decisively revealed in Christ, we have no reason to assume there is a particular divine reason behind every instance of suffering we confront. We certainly have no reason to assume that God is punishing people because of sin—he took care of that on Calvary—or that he's disciplining them to refine their character, though God will always *use* suffering to bring about whatever good he can.

We ordinarily can't know why particular individuals suffer the way they do. But in the light of God's revelation in Christ, our assumption should be that their suffering is something we should oppose in the name of God rather than accepting it as coming from God. Hence, the only relevant question disciples of Jesus should consider is, What can we do to bring God's redemptive will into the situation, to alleviate suffering and to glorify God? How can we respond in such a way that God's will is further accomplished "on earth as it is in heaven"? Instead of asking, "Who sinned?" we should ask, "How can we bring glory to God in this situation?" (Jn 9:1-3).

THE THEOLOGY OF JOB AND HIS FRIENDS

The only time the Bible makes an explicit connection between divine punishment and suffering in general is to deny that such a connection can be made. There is, as a matter of fact, an entire book of the Bible written to address this point. The central point of the book of Job is to teach us that the mystery of evil is a mystery of a war-torn and unfathomably complex creation, not the mystery of God's all-controlling will.

The prologue. Before discussing Job a few preliminary words need to be made. First, the genre of this book is epic poetry. As is customary with epic poems, it begins with a prologue that sets up the story line (chaps. 1-2). In Job the prologue gives the reader a perspective that the characters of the story lack. This is important, for the point of the whole narrative is to expose the vast ignorance of the characters involved.

The prologue centers on a dialogue that takes place between God and a certain rebel angel called (literally in Hebrew) "the *satan,*" meaning "the adversary." At this early stage of revelation (many scholars believe that Job is the oldest book of the Bible) this figure had not yet acquired "Satan" as a personal name. Though he is not yet seen as the altogether sinister cosmic force we find him to be in later biblical revelation, he is nevertheless depicted as somewhat outside of and in opposition to the Lord's authority.

The rebellious nature of the *satan* is alluded to in the prologue by the fact that he was not invited to the council meeting of the "heavenly beings" (literally, "sons of God," Job 1:6-7; 2:1). Indeed, the Lord seems surprised to see him. The Lord asks the *satan,* "Where have you come from?" To which the *satan* answers, "From going to and fro on the earth, and from walking up and down on it" (Job 1:7; 2:2). We see that the *satan* is not a being who operates according to the Lord's authority, as do the regular council members. He was not carrying out assignments from God. Rather, he randomly walks to and fro on the earth on his own. Indeed, the Lord has to protect people from him (1:10).

The *satan* assails God's wisdom and character by alleging that people only serve him because of what they get out of it. Their obedience, he is suggesting, isn't really a free choice. There is no genuine virtue in the world, the *satan* is claiming, only self-serving bargains, and obedience for the sake of being protected and blessed is one of these bargains. True holiness and virtuous obedience is an illusion. Take away a person's protection, the *satan* insists, and let him have his way with people, and they will stop living for God (Job 1:9-11; 2:4-5).

In the context of this narrative this assault can be refuted only by being put to a test. Were the Lord to simply force the *satan* into silence without proving him wrong, it would simply confirm the accuracy of the *satan's* charge: there is no integrity or wisdom in how God runs the universe; there's only raw power used to manipulate beings. People serve God only as a bargain, not out of genuine love.

The challenge has to be put to a test. God chooses the most righteous man on the earth to be tested. If Job fails, the narrative suggests, then the *satan* will have made his point. If Job succeeds, however, then God's wisdom and integrity in running the cosmos will be vindicated. Thus the protective fence around Job is removed and the *satan* is allowed to afflict him.

One final word about the prologue before we discuss the body of this work. Since we are dealing with an epic poem, most Old Testament scholars agree, it is misguided to press this prologue for literal details about God's general relationship to Satan. The literary point of the prologue is not to answer questions like "Does Satan always have to get specific permission every time he does something?" or "Is every affliction the result of a heavenly challenge to God's authority?" As with Jesus' parables the *central* point of the prologue is the *only* point the reader is supposed to get. We misunderstand Jesus' parable about Lazarus, for example, if we wonder whether people in hell can literally talk to people in paradise (Lk 16:19-31). The parable is simply a literary prop Jesus uses to make the point that people who don't repent on the basis of the revelation they've already received won't respond even if someone (like

Lazarus) came back from the dead (Lk 16:31).

The purpose of Job's prologue is to set up a specific episode that will vindicate God's wisdom and integrity. It serves this function by allowing the reader to see the *satan's* challenge to God while leaving the drama's characters in the dark. It thus highlights the characters' mistaken theological perspectives. It shows that things happen to people because of encounters in heaven about which these people know nothing. And this is the central point of the whole epic drama.

Job is to blame. The bulk of the narrative is formed around Job's conversations with his friends. Though his friends initially do the right thing and sit in silence (Job 2:13), when Job begins to express his pain, his friends begin to correct his theology. Sounding remarkably like many Christians today when they confront people in pain, and illustrating perfectly the complaint the *satan* originally raised against God, his friends insist that since God is perfectly just, Job must deserve what God is dishing out to him. People who serve God are protected and blessed, his friends assume, so they feel justified in concluding that those who clearly have not been protected and are not being blessed—people like Job—simply haven't been serving God. Job, therefore, is being disciplined.

Eliphaz is representative of this sort of blueprint wisdom when he says to Job:

Think now, who that was innocent ever perished?
    Or where were the upright cut off?
As I have seen, those who plow iniquity
    and sow trouble reap the same.
By the breath of God they perish,
    and by the blast of his anger they are consumed. (Job 4:7-9)

Of course, contra Eliphaz, we know that innocent and upright people are "cut off"—for example, sometimes babies die in the birthing process! Eliphaz's statements illustrate the remarkable capacity some people have to ignore reality for the sake of preserving a formulaic theology. As Job himself recognizes, his friends put forth their theology as a way of reassuring themselves that what happened to him couldn't happen to them (Job 6:20-21). They theologize out of their own fears, not as a way of ministering to Job in the midst of his needs. Surely the universe can't be as arbitrary as it seems, Job's friends insist. And in the process of reassuring themselves, they are indicting Job. For his unfortunate life doesn't conform to his friends' wishful-thinking theology.

Eliphaz continues: since God always does the right thing, and since both Job and his friends are assuming that God is directly behind what is happening to Job, Job should actually be happy about his plight. For it means that God is disciplining him for a good reason.

> How happy is the one whom God reproves;
> > therefore do not despise the discipline of the Almighty.
> For he wounds, but he binds up;
> > he strikes, but his hands heal. (Job 5:17-18)

This "encouragement" is being given to a man who just lost everything he owned, his health and his family! Yet, they insist, if Job would simply acknowledge that he is being justly disciplined, he would get his protection and blessing back from God.

> [God] will deliver you from six troubles;
> > in seven no harm shall touch you.
> In famine he will redeem you from death,
> > and in war from the power of the sword. . . .
> At destruction and famine you shall laugh,
> > and shall not fear the wild animals of the earth. . . .
> You shall know that your tent is safe,
> > you shall inspect your fold and miss nothing.
> You shall know that your descendants will be many,
> > and your offspring like the grass of the earth.

> You shall come to your grave in ripe old age,
>> as a shock of grain comes up to the threshing floor in its season.
> See, we have searched this out; it is true.
>> Hear, and know it for yourself." (Job 5:19-20, 22, 24-27)

As clichéd assurances often are, these words are self-serving and wounding. Promising a father who just lost all his children (Job 1:18-19) that if he will only get right with God his "tent" will be safe, his children will not be missing and his offspring will be like "the grass of the earth" is not just hollow, it's positively cruel. This is what Job's friends *want* to believe, for they want assurance that what happened to Job can't happen to them. But their wish-based theology is out of sync with reality and completely unhelpful to their suffering friend.

One of the central points of this profound book is to expose the shallowness of this popular theology. When God shows up to reveal the truth at the end of the book (Job 37—41), he doesn't concede that what happened to Job had anything to do with discipline or punishment. Indeed, God angrily rebukes Job's friends for speaking erroneously about God (Job 42:7).

This is not to say that everything Job's friends say about God is incorrect. This book is far too subtle to paint everything in either-or terms. It artfully paints a thoroughly ambiguous picture of the cosmos, where those who are basically in the wrong sometimes speak truth, and those whose hearts are basically right (Job) nevertheless speak many untruths, as seen in Job 42:7.[1] Yet the central point of the book's portrayal of the friends' "wisdom" to Job is that they speak out of massive ignorance.

Did the Lord bring about Job's trouble? The theology of Job's friends isn't the only theology this book aims at correcting. Though it is often missed, the author is intent on refuting Job's theology too. Against his friends Job insists that he is not more blameworthy than they or any other human being. But since he shares his friends' blueprint assumption that God is behind all that has happened to him, the only alternative conclusion available to him is that God is in fact arbitrary. When the Lord appears at the end of this book, he no more agrees with Job's theology than he agrees with the theology of his friends.

Toward the end of this book one verse has caused many to miss the point that the author refutes Job's theology as well as that of his friends. When the Lord is done speaking, the author notes that his friends consoled him for "the trouble the LORD had brought upon him" (Job 42:11 NIV). Several considerations prevent us from concluding that this verse implies Job was correct in seeing God as the cause of all his suffering.

First, while most ancient peoples believed that the world was fashioned and ruled by many conflicting gods, the Old Testament emphasizes that everything ultimately comes from one Creator God. To drive home this highly distinctive belief, Old Testament authors consistently emphasize that God is the *ultimate source* of everything that happens in creation. Even the consequences of free decisions are in a sense brought about by the Creator, in their view, for he alone created the people (and angels) who make real decisions.

More specifically, the Lord is depicted in terms of an ancient Near Eastern monarch who takes responsibility for what his delegates do, even if they don't carry out his own wishes. An authority's delegates are, in a sense, an extension of himself.[2] In a context where the singularity of the cosmic monarch needs to be emphasized, such as the Old Testament, the autonomy of subordinate delegates is minimized and the Creator's authority is maximized. In this sense, everything humans and angels do is seen as coming from God.

Understood in the ancient Near Eastern context, this doesn't mean that everything agents do happens *in accordance with God's will* or that God is himself *morally* responsible for what the agents he creates choose to do. For, as we saw in chapter three, the heavenly and human agents the Lord creates are the originators of their own free decisions, and they are morally responsible for these decisions. God is the ultimate source of their freedom, and he takes responsibility for the cosmos as a whole. But the agents themselves decide how they will use this God-given freedom. Thus to say in this context that something came from the Lord via another agent is not to say that this thing was part of God's own plan, that he directly brought it about or that he in any sense wills it (though as Creator he wills and brings about the *possibility* of evil deeds).

Second, Job 42:11 needs to be interpreted in light of the prologue, which clearly shows that it was the *satan*, not God, who afflicted Job. True, God entered into the wager with the *satan* and allowed him to afflict Job in order to answer the *satan's* assault on his integrity. In this sense he brought Job's troubles on him. But he did not himself plan or cause these afflictions, as Job later alleges. Indeed, as we noted above, the prologue goes out of its way to emphasize the haphazard nature by which Job's life is turned upside down. The *satan*, who wanders about on his own while causing mischief, just happens to show up at a heavenly council meeting. What happens to Job certainly is not part of God's perfect plan for his life!

Third, and even more important, we need to interpret Job 42:11 in the light of Jesus' ministry. Jesus is the central place where God's character and will are revealed. In Jesus' ministry people who suffered like Job were diagnosed as the direct or indirect victims of Satan's warfare against God. God's will isn't revealed in the afflictions Jesus encountered, but in his loving and powerful response to these afflictions.

Along the same lines, Christ's incarnation, death and resurrection reveal that though God is not culpable for the evil in the world, he nevertheless takes responsibility for it. And in taking responsibility for evil, he overcomes it. On the cross God suffers at the hands of evil. In this suffering and through his resurrection he destroys evil in principle. Through the cross and resurrection God unequivocally displays his loving character and establishes his loving purpose for the world despite its evil resistance. He thereby demonstrates that evil is not something he wills *into* existence: it's something he wills *out of* existence.

Fourth, the most decisive indicator that the author intends to refute

Job's theology is that the Lord never acknowledges that he is the one behind Job's suffering. Instead, God appeals to factors *in creation* to explain why Job can't understand his suffering.

Job gets the point. When God is done talking, Job confesses, "I have uttered what I did not understand" (Job 42:3), and he repents (v. 6). However we interpret Job 42:11, it can't be taken to endorse a theology the Lord refutes and Job repents of.

Job's misguided theology. A final indication that the author doesn't endorse Job's theology is that few of us could embrace some of Job's observations even though they logically flow from the assumption that God is behind Job's suffering. For example, throughout the narrative Job depicts God as a cruel tyrant who controls everything in an arbitrary fashion. Job exclaims:

When disaster brings sudden death,
    [God] mocks at the calamity of the innocent.
The earth is given into the hand of the wicked;
    He covers the eyes of its judges—
    If it is not he, who then is it?
        (Job 9:23-24, cf. 21:17-26, 30-32; 24:1-12)

God laughs at the misfortunes of the innocent and causes judges to judge unjustly! Can anyone imagine a biblical author *endorsing* this perspective? Of course not. But it gets worse.

Why are times not kept by the Almighty?
    And why do those who know him never see his days? (Job 24:1)

What is the Almighty, that we should serve him?
        And what profit do we get if we pray to him?' (21:15)

From the city the dying groan,
        And the throat of the wounded cries for help;
        Yet God pays no attention to their prayer. (24:12)

The victims of injustice—which God himself is bringing about—cry for help, but God pays no attention to their prayers. Is this the view the author is recommending in contrast to the theology of Job's friends?

Job's depiction of God is even harsher when he considers the injustice of his own life. For example, Job cries out to the Lord:

Your hands fashioned and made me;
> And now you turn and destroy me. (Job 10:8)

Bold as a lion you hunt me;
> you repeat your exploits against me . . .
> Let me alone; that I might find a little comfort. (10:16, 20)

You have turned cruel to me;
> with the might of your hand you persecute me. (30:21)

And to his friends Job testifies:

God has worn me out;
> he has made desolate all my company.
And he has shriveled me up . . .
He has torn me in his wrath, and hated me;
> He has gnashed his teeth at me;
> my adversary sharpens his eyes against me.
> (Job 16:7-9, cf. 11-17)

With violence he seizes my garment;
> He grasps me by the collar of my tunic. (30:18)

Are we to believe that these are theological insights the author is recommending? Should we view God as our adversary instead of our advocate (cf. Jn 14:16, 26; 15:26; 16:7; 1 Jn 2:1)? Is comfort found when God leaves us alone (Job 10:20) rather than when he is with us? Doesn't the god Job describes in these passages sound much more like "a roaring lion . . . looking for someone to devour"—in other words, "your adversary the devil" (1 Pet 5:8)? Of course he does, which is why Job later confesses, "I have uttered what I did not understand" (Job 42:3) and proclaims, "I despise myself, and repent in dust and ashes" (Job 42:6).

People often quote Job's words "the LORD gave and the LORD has taken away" (Job 1:21) when someone, like Melanie, has lost someone precious to them. As we saw in chapter one, the man whose wife killed his five children uttered these words at his children's funeral—as though God, not his wife, took the lives of his children. The irony is that though these words are spoken from an honest and upright heart, they are part of a theology Job *repents* of. Though Job initially "did not sin or charge God with wrongdoing" (Job 1:22), this theology ultimately leads Job—as it did Melanie—to complete despair. Before long, Job works out with ruthless clarity the implications of what he believes.

When the despairing Job complains, "Your hands fashioned and made me; and now you turn and destroy me" (Job 10:8), isn't he articulating in less pious terms his earlier, "the Lord gave and the Lord has taken away"? Though his willingness to submit changes to rage as his despair deepens, *his view of God remains the same.* For Job the god who arbitrarily gives and takes away is a capricious destroyer, a vicious predator, an adversary of humanity, the source of all suffering and injustice, a mocker of the innocent, and a god who doesn't heed the prayer of those in need.

This definitely is *not* the view of God the author of this inspired book is commending to his readers. But it's Job's view, and it's completely consistent with the assumption, shared by his friends, that God is behind all adversity in life.

THE MYSTERY OF AN UNFATHOMABLY COMPLEX CREATION

The straightness of Job's heart. When God sets the record straight, providing us with a three-chapter climax of this book, he corrects the thinking of both Job and his friends (Job 38—41). Job passes his test not because his theology is correct but because he does not reject God *even when his theology tells him he should.* Despite his theological misconceptions and impious rantings, Job's heart remains honest with God. His friends' theology usually sounds much more pious, but their hearts are actually further from God than Job's. In the words of John Gibson:

> Of course God did not approve of everything that his proud and litigious servant had said about him (his speeches from the whirlwind have made that abundantly clear), but he . . . infinitely preferred Job's attacks on him to the friends' defense of him.[3]

Job speaks straight from the heart about God, while his friends speak in self-serving ways (Job 42:7). Not only this, but Job works out his theology with ruthless consistency. If God were in fact the all-controlling deity Job assumed him to be, then the terrible conclusions he draws about God are right.[4] Yet despite this false conception of God, Job doesn't reject him in his heart. Against the charge of the *satan*, Job thereby proves that people do worship God of their own free will—just because God is God, not because there's something in it for them.

Vastness and complexity of creation. Still, God corrects Job's theology. In the concluding speeches God no more acknowledges Job's perspective than he does the friends' perspective. Rather, he refutes *both* perspectives by alluding to two facts: human ignorance about the vastness and complexity of the cosmos, and human ignorance about the enormity of chaos that God must contend with.

To highlight the first fact, the Lord asks Job, "Who is this that darkens counsel by words without knowledge?" (Job 38:2) and "Where were you when I laid the foundation of the earth?" (Job 38:4). And he continues:

> Who determined its measurements—surely you know!
>> Or who stretched the line upon it?
> On what were its bases sunk,
>> or who laid its cornerstone
> when the morning stars sang together
>> and all the heavenly beings shouted for joy? (Job 38:5-7)

Have you comprehended the expanse of the earth?
Declare, if you know all this. (38:18)

What is the way to the place where the light is distributed,
or where the east wind is scattered upon the earth? (38:24)

Do you know the ordinances of the heavens?
Can you establish their rule on the earth? (38:33)

The point of these questions is to expose the massive ignorance of Job and his friends. The Lord is putting all of them in their place to demonstrate how arrogant it is for Job's friends to accuse Job and for Job to accuse God. We know so little about the vastness, complexity and ordinances of creation, we are in no position to accuse anyone. But note, the ignorance the Lord highlights in this passage is an ignorance *about creation*. Job's friends accuse Job, and Job accuses God, because they fail to humbly acknowledge their ignorance about the complexity of the world God has created.

Decision making and chaos theory. A recent development in science, chaos theory, helps illustrate the point God is making to Job. It highlights the interconnected complexity of life and the impossibility of our ever exhaustively comprehending it.[5]

Put in simplest terms, it has been demonstrated recently that the slightest variation in a sufficiently complex process at one point may cause remarkable variations in that process at another point. The flap of a butterfly wing in one part of the globe can be, under the right conditions, the decisive variable that brings about a hurricane in another part of the globe several months later. (This has been called "the butterfly effect.") To exhaustively explain why a hurricane (or any weather pattern, for that matter) occurs when and where it does, we'd have to know every detail about the past history of the earth—including every flap of every butterfly wing! Of course we can't ever approximate this kind of knowledge, which is why weather forecasting will always involve a significant degree of guesswork.

By analogy, this insight may be applied to free decisions. Because love requires choice, humans and angels have the power to affect others for better or worse. Indeed, every decision we make affects other agents in some measure. Sometimes the short-term effects of our choices are apparent, as in the way the decisions of parents immediately affect their children or the way decisions of leaders immediately affect their subjects. The long-term effects of our decisions are not always obvious, however. They are like ripples created by a rock thrown into a pond. Ripples endure long after the initial splash, and they interact with other ripples (the consequences of other decisions) in ways we could never have anticipated. And in certain circumstances, they may have a "butterfly effect." They may be the decisive variable that produces significant changes in the pond.

We might think of the overall state of the cosmos at any given moment as the total pattern of ripples made by a constant stream of rocks thrown into a pond. Each ripple interacts with other ripples, creating interference patterns. Every event and every decision of history creates such an interference pattern. This intersection of multitudes of decisions contributes to all subsequent interference patterns.

Each person influences history by using his or her morally responsible say-so, creating ripples that affect other agents. And as the originators and ultimate explanation for their own decisions, individuals bear primary responsibility for the ripples they create. Yet each individual is also influenced by the whole. Decisions others have made affect their lives, and these people were themselves influenced by decisions others made. In this sense every event is an interference pattern of converging ripples extending back to Adam, and each decision we make influences the overall interference pattern that affects subsequent individuals.

From this it should be clear that to explain in any exhaustive sense why a particular event took place just the way it did, we would have to know the entire history of the universe. Had any agent, angelic or human, made a different decision, the world would be a slightly different—

or perhaps significantly different—place. But we, of course, can never know more than an infinitesimally small fraction of these previous decisions, let alone why these agents chose the way they did. Add to this our massive ignorance of most natural events in history—which also create their own ripples—combined with our ignorance of foundational physical and spiritual laws of the cosmos, and we begin to see why we experience life as mostly ambiguous and highly arbitrary. We are the heirs to an incomprehensibly vast array of human, angelic, and natural ripples throughout history about which we know next to nothing but which nevertheless significantly affect our lives.

Using a language Job could understand, this was essentially the point God was making in his first speech. We finite humans have no means of knowing the innumerable variables that would explain why things happen as they do. Whether we are speaking of human decisions, angelic decisions or the flap of butterfly wings, creation is too vast and complex for us to get our minds around. Yet every detail affects the course of things in at least a small way. Hence we experience life as largely arbitrary.

In the end the question, "Why me?"—or "Why Job?"—is unanswerable. It's a mystery. But the point of the book of Job, and a lesson we can appropriate from chaos theory, is that this isn't a mystery about God's will or character; it's a mystery about the vastness and complexity of *creation*. We experience life as arbitrary simply because we are finite. And when we try to arrogantly deny this finitude by ignoring all we don't know about creation, we end up either indicting people (as Job's friends did) or indicting God (as Job did). What we learn from this profound book is that the reason why Job—as opposed to someone else—suffered as he did had nothing to do with his sinful character or God's arbitrary character. Rather, Job's suffering resulted from a confrontation in the heavenly realm between God and an adversary that no one in the context of the narrative knew anything about.

When all is said and done, the mystery of why any particular misfortune befalls one person rather than another is no different than the mystery of why *any* particular event happens the way it does. Every particular thing we think we understand in creation is engulfed in an infinite sea of mystery we can't understand. The mystery of the particularity of evil is simply one manifestation of the mystery of every particular thing.

THE MYSTERY OF RESISTING COSMIC FORCES

The war that engulfs creation. The second fact God alludes to in correcting Job and his friends concerns the warfare that engulfs creation. Peoples of the ancient Near East depicted cosmic evil as either hostile waters or cosmic creatures ("Behemoth" in Job 40 and "Leviathan" in Job 41) who threatened to destroy the world. This was their way of identifying demonic "principalities and powers," and it's found throughout the Bible (e.g., Job 3:8; 9:13; 26:12; Ps 74:14; 87:4, 89:10; Is 27:1; 51:9).[6] In order to make his point to Job in a language Job could understand, the Lord reminds Job of the Lord's battle with both the raging sea and the cosmic monsters. Regarding the cosmic sea the Lord says,

> Who shut in the sea with doors
>   when it burst out from the womb . . .
> and prescribed bounds for it,
>   and set bars and doors,
> and said, "Thus far shall you come, and no farther,
>   and here shall your proud waves be stopped"? (Job 38:8, 10-11)

The Lord is reminding Job of the hostile sea that all ancient Near Eastern people believed must be kept at bay if the order of the world was to be preserved. Until Job thinks he can do a better job than God, he should be reticent to follow the *satan's* lead and challenge God's character and ability in running the cosmos.

Concerning Leviathan, the Lord asks Job, "Can you draw out Leviathan with a fishhook, or press down its tongue with a cord?" (Job 41:1). Only the Lord can contend with this malevolent creature (though even he needs a sword! [Job 40:19]), for this cosmic beast is indeed ferocious.

Its sneezes flash forth light,
    and its eyes are like the eyelids of the dawn.
From its mouth go flaming torches;
    sparks of fire leap out.
Out of its nostrils comes smoke,
    as from a boiling pot and burning rushes.
Its breath kindles coals,
    and a flame comes out of its mouth . . .
It counts iron as straw,
    and bronze as rotten wood. (Job 41:18-21, 27)

This cosmic beast fears nothing (Job 41:33). It cannot be captured or domesticated (Job 41:1-8). Even "the gods" are "overwhelmed at the sight of it" (Job 41:9, 25). And no one "under heaven" can "confront it and be safe" (Job 41:11). The Lord emphasizes the ferociousness of this beast not to call into question his own ability to handle it but to stress to Job that this foe is indeed formidable. The battle the Lord is engaged in is not a charade.[7]

By reminding Job of the cosmic forces he must contend with, God again exposes the simplistic theologies of both Job and his friends. Neither considered the warfare that engulfs creation. Both simply assumed that things unfold the way the Lord wants them to. God's appeal to this warfare alters these theologies considerably. It means that not everything happens exactly as the Lord would wish. God himself must battle forces of chaos.

Fredrik Lindstöm, an eminent Old Testament scholar, sums up the matter well when he writes:

> [The Lord] in fact partially admits to Job that there are parts of Creation which are indeed chaotic; here we catch sight of an understanding of the world in which evil... neither comes directly from God, as Job maintains, nor can it be accommodated to a world order in which it is ultimately related to human behavior, as Job's friends claim.[8]

And again:

> Job explicitly held [the Lord] responsible for all the evil of exis-
> tence, so [the Lord] rebuts this charge by pointing to his own con-
> tinuous combat with evil as manifested in these chaos creatures.[9]

The cosmos is far more complex and combative than either Job or his
friends had assumed.

Another eminent Old Testament scholar, John Gibson, expresses the
point even more forcefully. He notes that "chapters 40 and 41 do not
mention an open victory of God over Behemoth and Leviathan, but simply describe them as they are in their full horror and savagery." From this
he concludes that the central point of these chapters is to draw attention

> to the Herculean task God faces in controlling these fierce creatures
> of his in the here and now. They are in fact set forth as worthy op-
> ponents of their Creator. They are quite beyond the ability of men to
> take on and bring to book. On the contrary, they treat men with
> scorn and derision, delighting to tease and humiliate and terrorize
> them. . . . [E]ven God has to watch for them and handle them with
> kid gloves. It takes all his "craft and power" to keep them in subjec-
> tion and prevent them from bringing to naught all that he has
> achieved. . . . It is of this divine risk as well as of the divine grace and
> power that Job is . . . being given an intimation in Yahweh's second
> speech: of the terrible reality of evil and (as Job himself was now only
> too well aware) of the dangers it presents to men.[10]

The point of the Lord's second speech—the foundation of which was
laid in the prologue—is that human lives are affected by "behind the
scenes" events that resist God's providential control. We know and can
do next to nothing about these happenings. We therefore experience life
as an arbitrary flux of fortune and misfortune.

The fact that neither Job nor his friends are told about the *satan* who
began the whole mess reinforces this point. After the prologue the *satan*
isn't mentioned again. The main characters of this epic poem never learn

what the reader knew all along. And this is precisely the point of the book. We don't know and can't know why particular harmful events unfold exactly as they do. What we *can* know, however, is *why* we can't know: it's not because God's plan or character is mysterious but because we are finite humans in an *incomprehensibly vast creation* that is afflicted by forces of chaos. The mystery of the particularity of evil, which is no different than the mystery of the particularity of everything, is located in the mystery of creation, not the mystery of God. And given this mystery, we must refrain from blaming each other or blaming God when misfortunes arise. Rather, following the example of Jesus, we must simply ask, What can we do in response to the evil we encounter?

Western Christians rarely take seriously the reality of the spirit world as a variable that affects their lives. We ordinarily assume that God's will and human faith are the only two relevant variables that decide what comes to pass. So, for example, when we pray and our request doesn't come to pass, we typically conclude that it must not have been God's will, or that the person praying lacked faith or didn't pray hard enough. The book of Job, the ministry of Jesus and the Bible in general suggest that such formulaic thinking misses the complexity of the real world and is therefore dangerous for just this reason.

A delay in Daniel's prayer. One of the most intriguing and graphic illustrations of the significance of the spirit world is found in the book of Daniel. For three weeks Daniel fasts and prays to hear from God, with no answer (Dan 10:3). Finally, an angel appears to him and says:

> Do not fear, Daniel, for from the first day that you set your mind to gain understanding and to humble yourself before your God, your words have been heard, and I have come because of your words. But the prince of the kingdom of Persia opposed me twenty-one days. So Michael, one of the chief princes, came to help me, and I left him there with the prince of the kingdom of Persia. (Dan 10:12-13)

The delay in answering Daniel's prayer has nothing to do with God's will or Daniel's lack of faith. It was due to the interference of a demonic spirit called "the prince of the kingdom of Persia." Because God's purpose in creation is love, he wants to carry out his will through agents who choose to love and obey him. Thus he usually works through mediators on both a physical and spiritual level. And what happens to these mediators affects the way God's will is carried out. When they align themselves with God's purposes, things go smoothly. But when they set themselves in opposition to God's will, such as the territorial spirit over Persia had done, God's will is disrupted. Only after the angel Michael helps the angel who was dispatched is Daniel's prayer answered.

Not only this, but after arriving the angel tells Daniel why he (the angel) has to leave quickly.

> Now I must return to fight against the prince of Persia, and when I am through with him, the prince of Greece will come. . . . There is no one with me who contends against these princes except Michael, your prince. (Dan 10:20-21)

It seems that Michael needed help in battling the spiritual powers that opposed God. Perhaps there were no other angels on God's side available to aid Michael. People often assume that God has an unlimited number of angels available to him. But Scripture suggests that the nature of things in the spiritual realm is not much different than the nature of things in our physical realm. Because God has chosen to work through physical and spiritual mediators who are finite in number and strength, battles are influenced by the number and strength of agents fighting for or against his purposes (for more on this see chapter seven).

Through this episode we gain a rare glimpse of behind-the-scenes events that affect our lives. Had the angel not revealed this information to Daniel, Daniel would never have known why it took twenty-one days to answer him. It would have seemed totally arbitrary. No doubt some would have followed Job's lead and said, "It must not be God's will" or, "God's timing is the best timing." Others, like Job's friends, would have concluded, "Daniel must lack faith or must not be righteous." But the delay had nothing to do with either of these variables. It had to do with agents in the spiritual realm who possess say-so and who use it to either further or resist God's purposes. Like humans, angels create ripples that create interference patterns with other ripples for better or for worse. Yet we know even less about angelic ripples than we know about human ripples.

CONCLUSION

Most of us don't like ambiguity. Life is generally easier when we believe that everything is clear and simple. This, I believe, is part of our legacy of eating of the tree of the knowledge of good and evil. In our fallen delusion, we believe it's our right and within our capacity to declare unambiguously who and what are "good" or "evil." We aren't omniscient, but having eaten from the forbidden tree, we have a misguided impulse to judge matters *as though we were*. We have difficulty accepting our finitude and the massive ignorance and ambiguity attached to it.

In point of fact, however, creation can be only experienced by finite beings as unfathomably complex and therefore mostly ambiguous. We have no means of ascertaining more than a minute fraction of the variables that factor into each event within this unfathomably complex creation. This isn't because we are fallen: it's simply because we are finite. This is why our original job description—which God is yet calling us to fulfill—involves very little knowing but a great deal of loving. Our limited domain of responsibility is primarily to love God and others as we are filled with God's love. Hence the Bible repeatedly calls us to love and to refrain from judgment (Mt 7:1-5; Rom 2:1-5; Jas 4:11-12).[11]

Because of our addiction to the forbidden fruit, however, we want to know and judge. If our finite knowledge can't adjust to the complexity of reality, we simply try to readjust the complexity to our finite capacity to know. Hence we bracket off the complexity of reality and act as if things were simple enough for us to understand.

This is why many people are compulsively inclined to judge others on the basis of surface behavior, bracketing off the vast complexity of variables that affect and perhaps explain this perceived behavior. Though the Bible expressly forbids it, pretending that we know and thus can judge a person's heart gives us a sense of ethical superiority and personal security. And this is also why we are inclined toward simplistic, formulaic theologies. Like Job's friends and Job himself, we feel secure when we bracket off the complexity and ambiguity, and convince ourselves that the world unfolds according to a divine blueprint. We assume that everything can be explained by appealing to God's will or the wills of people.

This theology works only so long as we can in fact bracket off reality. But when reality in all its unfathomable complexity and war-torn horror encroaches on us, as it did on Melanie, victims suffer and so does our theology. When we compromise what we *do* know (God revealed in Jesus Christ) because we forget what we *don't* know (the complex creation)—when we make the mystery of evil a mystery about God rather than creation—we tarnish God's character and indict victims of the war. As depicted in the book of Job, some blame God, others blame people. But as the book of Job teaches us, both responses are fundamentally mistaken.

A healthier perspective, one which honors God's character revealed in Christ and refrains from indicting people, acknowledges ambiguity and warfare up front. We must with confidence anchor ourselves in what we can know—that God looks like Jesus—and simply confess ignorance about everything else.

If we are going to blame anyone, the book of Job and the ministry of Jesus would have it be Leviathan, Behemoth, hostile cosmic waters or (what comes to the same thing) the devil. Though we can't know the "why" of any particular instance of suffering, we can and must know that our whole environment is under siege by forces that hate God and all that is good. By our own rebellion we are caught in the crossfire of a cosmic war, and we suffer accordingly.

In chapter three I argued that we can understand why the *possibility* of evil is necessary in a creation in which love is the goal. In this chapter, however, I have argued that we can never fully understand why evil is *actualized* the way it is. What is crucial for us to see, however, is that this mystery doesn't surround God's character, will or purpose. Rather, it's a mystery that necessarily surrounds an unimaginably complex creation that has become a war zone. The one thing we can be confident of in this otherwise ambiguous world is the character and will of God. This confidence is derived from our resolve to keep our eyes fixed on Jesus Christ.

FIVE

OMNIPOTENCE AND
TWO VARIABLES

In the last chapter I argued that the mystery of evil is about the unfathomable complexity and war-torn nature of the cosmos; it's not about God's character, purpose or will. We can know who God is in Jesus Christ, but we can know very little about creation. We can't in any comprehensive sense know why any particular event happens the way it does. There are far too many unknowable variables that would need to be factored in to such knowledge. Indeed, to know *anything* exhaustively, we'd have to know *everything* exhaustively.

THE QUESTION OF SUPERNATURAL INTERVENTION

The reality of agents' say-so. Whether we are talking about a particular child dying at birth or a duck landing on a particular pond at a particular moment, we can never fully know why things happen the way they do. The perennial question "Why me?" is no different than the question "Why did this duck land in this pond at just this moment?" It is strictly unanswerable from a finite human perspective. For all we know, had a butterfly flapped its wing differently in the seventh century, the duck would have shown up next week instead of now.

People operating out of the blueprint model typically want to discount this complexity as irrelevant. They may grant there are an unfathomable number of unknowable variables that influence what comes to pass. But *ultimately* all things happen because God thought it better to have them happen (or to allow them to happen) than not. I have argued that this perspective is at odds with the picture of God we get in Jesus Christ, and with the reality of human and angelic free will presupposed throughout Scripture and in our everyday life.

To have say-so means that the explanation for our choices lies within ourselves, and thus we are ultimately responsible for the effect these choices have on ourselves and others. Not everything happens because God wills it or specifically allows it. Agents will many things even though God doesn't. God has a reason why he creates agents free, but he doesn't necessarily have a reason for why agents freely make the particular decisions they make.

God is infinitely intelligent, of course, and thus is able to perfectly anticipate a response to each decision. In this sense he *assigns* a reason to each decision *after the fact*.[1] What others intend for evil, God intends for good (Gen 50:20). But the reason why the decision was made in the first place ultimately lies within the agent, not God.

Life is arbitrary because of the way the decisions made by an unfathomably vast multitude of free agents intersect with each other. It is not a function of God's will or character.

What role does God play? This raises an extremely important practical question. Given the vast influence of all the angelic and human wills God created, what influence does God have in determining what comes to pass? Yes, he has an important role to play in anticipating and creatively responding to decisions agents make. But is God *only* a responder? If the blueprint model errs in ascribing the ultimate reason for *everything* to God, it might seem that the warfare model errs in not ascribing the ultimate reason for *anything* to God.

The question is extremely important on a number of accounts, not least of which is that Christianity is founded on the assumption that God can and does unilaterally intervene in the affairs of humans. The biblical portrait of God is of one who responds to events. He is a God who at times supernaturally intervenes to alter the course of history and of individual lives.

Taking Jesus Christ as our starting point, we can't avoid concluding that God intervenes in the world. Indeed, Jesus is the supreme instance of God intervening in human affairs. In Christ God became a human! If that doesn't constitute supernatural intervention, nothing does! As God in human form, Christ himself is the decisive refutation of any theology that brackets off the influence of God from the cosmos.

Christ's ministry was centered on demonstrating God's supernatural power in counteracting the tragic effects of the kingdom of darkness. He announced the kingdom of God was at hand and proved it by supernaturally healing and delivering people from demonic oppression. And he taught us to pray that his Father's will be done "on earth as it is in heaven." The rest of the biblical narrative concurs with this perspective, for it is woven around miracles that God performed on behalf of his people, often in response to prayer. From the parting of the Red Sea to the miracles of the early church, the Bible witnesses to a miracle-working God.

From a Christ-centered, biblical perspective, God's ability to break into history is the foundation of our confidence in him. If God can part the Red Sea, become a human being, die on a cross and rise from the dead, then we can trust him to intervene and redeem today's tragic circumstances. Even more fundamentally, we can trust that he will someday vanquish all his foes once and for all, bring this present age to a close, and set up a kingdom of love that will never end. We are confident that things will not always go on as they are precisely because God is not bound to the natural processes.

Why the arbitrariness? The same miracle-working power that gives hope to the believer also raises a multitude of questions. Chief among these is, Why does God's intervention in the world seem so arbitrary? Yes, God can heal blindness. But why does God heal one blind person and not another?

These sorts of questions have led many to embrace the blueprint world-view. The reasoning goes something like this: If God can heal one blind man at one time, it seems he could heal *any* blind man *any* time. Thus it seems the reason many remain blind is because God is unwilling to heal them. And if he's unwilling to heal them, it must be his will they remain blind. Hence, whether a person is born blind or with sight and whether he or she remains blind or is healed is all part of God's "secret plan." This line of reasoning is then applied to all diseases and personal tragedies. There-fore, it is concluded, *whatever* happens must be because God wants it to happen—or at least because God didn't want to stop it from happening.

Clearly, if this is true, all talk about the complexity and war-torn na-ture of the cosmos is quite irrelevant. From the blueprint perspective, God can trump the effect of free will any time he wants to. Thus, if free will has any influence on what comes to pass, it's because God has al-lowed it. Which means that the ultimate reason is found *in God*, not in the free agents.

Something's amiss. This line of reasoning is simple, logical and, for many, reassuring. Yet I think it is fundamentally misguided. The conclu-sion it leads to is not shared by Christ (see chapter two). It runs against the entire warfare motif and free-will emphasis found in Scripture (see chapter three). And if we hold fast to our faith that God is perfectly good and loving, the blueprint worldview requires that every horrifying aspect of creation somehow makes the cosmos as a whole a better place! But when we enter into the nightmare of one screaming, tortured child— and it is our duty to think through our faith from such a perspective— we can understand why many conclude God is not perfectly good or lov-ing, or that he doesn't exist at all.

This line of reasoning is misguided in assuming that the only variable that affects what God can do is his own will. It simplistically assumes that if God can work supernaturally *at all,* he must work supernaturally *always.* It's misguided because it has forgotten the complexity and war-torn nature of the cosmos, and it compromises what we know about God in Christ. If we think about the matter carefully, we'll see that God sometimes supernaturally intervenes and other times doesn't because of creation's complexity.

To make my case, I'll first argue that claiming God can't do something doesn't necessarily deny his omnipotence, as many assume. Then I'll flesh out two variables in this kind of world that affect and restrict what God can do in any particular situation. This perspective renders intelligible the biblical truths that God *does* intervene to alter the course of events but that he *can't* always do this.

CAN'T VERSUS WON'T

The question we are wrestling with ultimately comes down to this: Why doesn't God intervene to prevent evil more often? Is it because he doesn't want to? or because he can't? If we say it's because he doesn't want to, we have to accept the blueprint worldview. This usually has been accepted as the only viable option because saying God *can't* do something seems to deny his omnipotence. Moreover, Scripture clearly teaches that God is able to do things we ordinarily think can't be done (i.e., miracles).

Nevertheless, in the light of the problems with the "won't" option, we need to revisit the "can't" option. Whether this option conflicts with God's omnipotence and Scripture depends entirely on what we mean when we say God can't do something.

Doing the logically impossible. Everyone who gives the matter much thought grants that God *can't* do something that is logically contradictory, for there is no meaning in asserting that he *can* do something logically contradictory. God can't create round triangles or a married bachelor, for example. A triangle is something that is noncircular, and a bachelor is a man who is not married. To ascribe to God the ability to do such things is nonsensical. A logical contradiction doesn't become a compliment just because it's attributed to God!

I make the same point when I say that whatever God does, he does *it* and *not something else.* If God decides to create any particular thing, he thereby decides *not* to create it as any other particular thing. *What God creates is what it is by virtue of not being anything else.* This means that in deciding to create something as it is, God *can't* decide to create it other than it is. His decision to create a triangle rules out making it at the same time a circle, and his decision to create a bachelor rules out making, at the same time, that same person married.[2]

The logical constraints on the Creator. We tend to attribute the arbitrariness of God's intervention in the world to God rather than to the complexity of creation because we have not applied this rule of logic to God's role as Creator. We have too quickly opted for the blueprint perspective because we have failed to appreciate that in creating one kind of world God thereby ruled out any other kind of world.

To be more specific, God could have created a world in which his will is always done. Had he chosen to do so, however, a world in which his will is possibly *not* done would have been ruled out. Thus he would have ruled out a world in which other agents make free choices. And if my contention that love requires choice is correct (see chapter three), this means he would have ruled out a world where love is possible. (Remember, God can't create a round triangle.)

Conversely, if God decided to create a world where love *is* possible, he thereby ruled out a world in which his will is always done. If he chooses to create this kind of world, he can't guarantee that his will is always done, not because he lacks power but *because of the kind of world he created.* Just as a triangle can't be round, so too a world that includes love can't guarantee that God's will always comes to pass.

There is no reason to avoid saying God *can't* do something so long as we are clear that this "can't" is the logical consequence of *decisions God made.* The reason God's intervention in the world appears arbitrary is because of the variables in *this* kind of world. He can't intervene more than he does, not because he lacks power but because the kind of world he created prevents him from doing so. But what is it about the kind of world God created that allows him to intervene some times but prevents him at others, even though he has the sheer power to intervene at all times?

If we think through the implications of God's decision to create the kind of world in which love is possible, we begin to understand why God can supernaturally intervene some times, but not at others. There are a number of necessary variables in a world where love is possible. The remainder of this chapter examines two variables of creation that shape how God acts in the world.[3] The next chapter will examine a third. These variables affect and restrict what the omnipotent God can do at any particular time.

A final preliminary word. In discussing these two variables I am not claiming that *in any particular instance* we can know why God could or couldn't supernaturally alter a situation. Apart from divine revelation it's impossible for us finite beings to know this. All I am attempting to do is flesh out two kinds of things that affect what God can do in this complex and war-torn world he created.

VARIABLE 1: THE NECESSARY ORDER OF THE WORLD

The need for a stable medium. Love requires relationships. If God's goal is love, creation must be conducive to building relationships. People need a common medium in which to relate to one another. This medium is our physical environment—our world. We relate to each other by using our physical bodies in our physical environment.

To illustrate, in order to communicate to you right now, I am using my body (beginning with the neurons in my brain and extending to my fingers) to record my thoughts on my computer. These thoughts eventually are transferred to the pages of this book. The light bouncing off these words then impacts your eyes and ultimately ends up stimulating the neurons in your brain that (hopefully) decode the sensations to have roughly the same meaning I have. If you are following what I'm writing right now, I have related to you through the shared medium of our physical environment.

Relationships are only possible when (1) all parties can *influence* others by influencing their environment, and (2) no party can exhaustively *control* others or their environment. If I exhaustively controlled the environment, then you couldn't freely influence it to relate to other people. In other words, our shared medium must be pliable enough for us to influence it but resistant enough that no one can exhaustively control it.

For the physical world to operate this way, it has to be governed by "laws."[4] Imagine how difficult (impossible!) it would be for us to relate to each other if we couldn't count on the laws of nature remaining the same from one day to the next. We can relate to one another and influence the world because the laws of nature are stable and regular. This makes our environment both pliable and resistant.

What has this got to do with God? Simply this: if God wants a world in which agents can relate to one another, he must create a world that is very stable and thus quite predictable. In deciding to create this kind of world, God ruled out a world in which the laws of nature could be altered every time someone was going to be harmed. If the laws could be suspended on a regular basis, life would be chaotic. There would be no stability in which to create relationships. But the knife cuts two ways. For example, while the law of gravity allows us to relate to one another on the earth, it also can harm us if our parachute doesn't open.

It is also true that the regularity of the world doesn't have to be *absolutely* uniform. As Creator, God certainly has the power and the right to "suspend" the regularity of the world at any time. But he can't do this all the time, or even most of the time, if he wants us to have stable, nonchaotic lives. Because of the kind of world God decided to create, he can intervene on occasion, but not at all times.

What we don't know. Of course, we have no clear idea how regular, stable and predictable the world must be for us to relate at the level God wants us to. Thus we don't know how much God can override the stability of the world without compromising it. And we certainly don't know why God decides to override the world's regularity some times, but not others. This means that we can't know how this variable applies *in any particular instance.*

However, what we can know is significant. In creating a stable, non-chaotic world, God ruled out a world in which he could intervene any time, place or manner he desires. Though God's power is unlimited, the extent to which he can use it to suspend the regularity of the world is not. This is what it means for God when he created a stable world in which we can relate to one another.

VARIABLE 2: THE IRREVOCABILITY OF FREEDOM

The requirement of irrevocability. When God decided to create a world in which agents are capable of love, he also created one where agents are free not to love. Love involves choice. This means that God can't revoke agents' freedom when they act in unloving ways. If God were to revoke our freedom every time we used it in evil ways, we wouldn't be truly free.

Consider the matter this way: the difference between a free being and a predetermined being is that a free being is capable of choosing between options while a predetermined being is not. (Predetermined beings may *think* they have the power of choice, if they've been predetermined to think this way, but in fact they aren't genuinely *capable* of choosing.) Given two options, A and B, a free being is capable of choosing either one, whereas a predetermined being will "choose" the one he is predetermined to choose, let's say A. Now, if God revokes the ability of the free being to choose option B because he desires that being to choose A, then clearly the being was not free to choose A *or* B. She was, in fact, in the same position as the being who was predetermined to choose A. She was not free.

The illustration shows that to the extent that God genuinely gives freedom to any agent, he *has* to give it irrevocably. God *can't* intervene to stop it. He *has* to tolerate it. This isn't because God lacks the power to do so but because this what it means to give genuine freedom to agents. It's no different than saying when God creates a triangle, it must have three sides. When God gives freedom to agents, this freedom must be irrevocable.

This means that God must put up with the ongoing *effects* of agents' free decisions. Love is our capacity to make choices that bless people through time, and hate is our capacity to make choices that curse and damage people through time. This is our freedom as well as our moral say-so. We might say that options A and B will not just affect the present moment; they represent different and irrevocable splashes in a pond that will have a ripple effect for ages to come.

Qualifications of the irrevocable variable. This variable doesn't mean that God can *never* stop agents from engaging in certain actions. It simply means that *in so far as God has granted the agent freedom,* God can't revoke it to prevent the agent from truly choosing a course of action. Nor does it mean that God can't *influence* an agent's decision. It simply means that God's influence must respect the integrity of freedom given the agent, always stopping short of coercion.

This variable doesn't rule out *other agents* using their own freedom to prevent an agent's actions or from canceling the effects of that agent's decisions. Exercising this say-so may be part of their God-given freedom and responsibility. It may be that there are conditions that God places on the irrevocability of an agent's freedom or on the effects the agent creates. There may be a multitude of conditions that stipulate whether or not and to what extent an agent is free, or how long and under what circumstances the effects of free decisions are allowed to ripple in the pond.

However, to whatever extent agents have freedom and morally responsible say-so, they have it irrevocably. Neither free decisions nor their effects can be halted by God simply because they are not in line with his will.

Of course, God has always anticipated that agents will use their freedom the way they do, for he is infinitely intelligent and thus foresees every possibility as though it were a certainty. So he has a strategy to bring good out of any decision by influencing the situation to minimize its harmful effects. But this doesn't qualify the truth that God nevertheless has to tolerate free decisions and their effects.

We need to remind ourselves once again that *none of this concerns God's power.* To be sure, God has the power to revoke the freedom of Satan, his legions and every human being. But God's power is not the issue. The issue is the kind of world God decided to create and its logical implications. When God creates a triangle, it can't be round. And when God creates free agents, their freedom can't be revoked. Stated differently, when God gave agents freedom, he chose not to revoke their freedom if in the future they choose to use it against his will. These are not two separate decisions on God's part, but one. If God gives someone the power to choose A or B, this means God gives them the power to choose either one or the other. And A and B in this case are choices that will have a long-term impact on others, for better or for worse.

Is God to blame? A brief excursus is in order at this point. I have argued that God can't prevent all evil, not because he lacks power but because of the kind of world he chose to create. But couldn't a person nevertheless argue that God is still responsible for evil in the world? After all, he chose to limit himself by creating agents with irrevocable free will! Three things may be said in response to this claim.

First, we have no more reason to hold God morally responsible for the evil his creatures bring about than we do to hold parents morally responsible for the evil behavior of their adult children. An adult's free choice is the ultimate explanation of his or her own behavior, thus the adult child is morally responsible, not the parents. God cannot therefore be blamed for what free agents do, even though he is the one who gave them freedom.

Second, it nevertheless seems God could be held accountable for evil if the risk of creating this kind of world outweighed the gains. But why should we suppose this to be the case? Indeed, do finite beings have the vantage point from which to resolve this question? The only one who has a perspective broad enough to accurately assess whether the possible gains are worth the risk is God—and he has clearly deemed the risk of love worth it!

Even more fundamentally, don't we tacitly affirm the risk of love whenever we make ourselves vulnerable to others for the sake of love? Don't we implicitly acknowledge our agreement with God's decision every time we decide to bring children into the world? Isn't it true we are in fundamental agreement with God's decision whenever we are willing to put our lives or the lives of our children at risk to defend our freedom?

Indeed, we tacitly acknowledge that the risk of freedom is better than nonexistence simply by refraining from suicide each day. If we truly believed life with freedom is not worth the pain that comes with it, we would end it. That we continue to live and love suggests that it's more appropriate to praise than blame God for creating a world with free agents. At the core of our being we agree with God's decision to take the risk of freedom.

Third, and most important, though we have every reason to accept that God is not *morally culpable* for creating a world where evil occurs, we must remember that God nevertheless takes *responsibility* for evil. This is what the cross and resurrection of Jesus Christ are all about. God is not morally responsible for evil, but he voluntarily suffers the full force of evil in order to free creation from evil.

On the cross, Christ suffers *as though* he were morally culpable for evil. And in doing this, he in principle frees us from evil. The righteous One completely identifies with our sin so that we who are sinners might completely identify with his righteousness (2 Cor 5:21). Christ gives himself over to death that we who are dead might be given over to life. His victory over sin, death and the devil, evidenced by his rising from the dead, becomes our victory.

God takes responsibility for all that is wrong with his creation, not to purge himself, but us, of guilt. He graciously accepts responsibility for evil in order to free those who are responsible for evil.

What we don't know. To return to our central point: the degree to which God creates an agent with morally responsible say-so means, to that same degree, God gives that agent *irrevocable* say-so. This is why God can't simply intervene to stop (revoke) an agent's decision or its effects. It's also why we shouldn't suppose there is a specific reason why God allowed an agent to make a particular decision. The specific reason why agents do what they do lies within them, not God (Jer 4:14). I believe this variable explains a great deal about why God can't supernaturally alter the course of things whenever he pleases. But it does nothing to explain why *in any particular instance* God can or can't supernaturally alter events. For we have no idea how this variable applies in any particular instance.

We don't know how much irrevocable freedom God has granted to any individual and thus how much God has to tolerate the ongoing effects of that individual's evil choices. There is no reason to think God gives the same amount of freedom to everyone (it seems obvious he does not) or that the scope of this gift is fixed throughout a person's life (again, it seems obvious it is not). We can only know that to the extent that God has given free will, he can't revoke it.

In addition, we have no way of knowing what conditions are attached to any person's irrevocable freedom (or to the freedom of humans in general). Nor do we know the extent to which the ongoing impact of an agent's choices are irrevocable, or how long and under what conditions they will remain irrevocable. We don't know anything about how these irrevocable effects play out when they intersect with the effects of other decisions. Nor do we have any knowledge of how these effects qualify or constitute our own freedom, the rules by which God influences other agents to diminish these effects, the power God has granted to prayer to augment good and diminish bad effects (see chapter six), or even the fine line between God *influencing* an agent as opposed to *coercing* an agent. On all these matters we know next to nothing. But we can know that there *is* a significant degree of irrevocability in all this and that this conditions what God can and can't do in any given situation.

Our ignorance is actually much greater than this. We must remember that according to Scripture (and the intuitions of most people throughout history) spirit beings also have been given irrevocable freedom. Indeed, from what can be surmised from Scripture the domain of spirit beings' freedom, their morally responsible say-so, is generally far greater than that of most humans. Moreover, according to Scripture multitudes of these spirit beings have resolved to use their say-so to oppose God's plans and purposes.

God must also tolerate the effects of these angelic decisions. And many of these effects have significant impact on us. Scripture says we suffer under the tyranny of a "ruler" or "god" or "power" of this world (Jn 12:31; 14:30; 16:11; 2 Cor 4:4; Eph 2:2; 1 Jn 5:19). For this reason Jesus said sicknesses, diseases and infirmities are influenced by a rebellious spirit kingdom. And Scripture depicts Satan as the murderer who holds the power of death (Jn 8:44; Heb 2:14). Though we rarely if ever see it directly, we are significantly influenced by what goes on in the spiritual realm. Yet we know next to nothing about it.

Not only do we not know how much freedom these beings were originally given, but with few exceptions we don't know who they are, how many there are, where they are, how they operate or the "rules" that pertain to their mode of existence. We know next to nothing about spirit agents' decisions or what their long-term effects are. Nor do we know what effect prayer has on the activity of these beings, or what effect these beings have on our prayers in any particular instance—though we know from Scripture that there is an influence both ways. But we do know that to the extent that these spirit agents are free, God must tolerate and work around their decisions.

This is the best answer to why the omnipotent God has to engage in strategic warfare against spirit beings rather than simply obliterating them the moment they rebel. The duration of the cosmic war (which may be a mere blink of the eye to God, 2 Pet 3:8) is a testimony to the depth of freedom and morally responsible say-so God gave these agents.

At the same time, there is no reason to worry that this battle will rage on forever. Indeed, the resurrection of Jesus Christ and the whole of the biblical narrative testify to a future time when the say-so of all who oppose God will be used up, and God's love will rule creation. But until this time, God must work within the parameters of the kind of creation he chose to bring forth.

UNDERSTANDING THE ARBITRARINESS OF LIFE

The balance of constraints. Let's return to our original question: Why does God's interaction with us appear so arbitrary? So far we have discussed only two of many possible variables God must work with given his decision to create this kind of world, but I believe these two are sufficient to show that we need not appeal to God's will to answer this question.

The constraints God placed on himself by the necessity of a stable world order and by irrevocable freedom are strong enough to prevent God from *always* unilaterally intervening to prevent evil. But they aren't so strong that they prevent God from *sometimes* intervening. They are strong enough to allow agents to relate to one another and have morally responsible say-so. But they aren't so strong that the *only* thing that decides matters is the say-so of these agents. They are strong enough that his will *in particular cases* may be threatened. But they aren't so strong that his *overall* will for creation is threatened.

God sovereignly designed the world this way. He "set up the rules of the game," we might say. And even after we've learned a few (but only a few) of the general rules, the actual playing of the game appears arbitrary to us because we don't know how the rules apply in any particular instance. The complexity of the game is far beyond the comprehension of our finite minds.

A mother at the mall. An analogy may help illustrate our situation. Suppose you and a friend observe a mother with her three children shopping at a mall. Both of you are immediately puzzled at this mother's arbitrary behavior toward her children. She originally gives unequal amounts of money to two of her children and takes money away from the third. As the day progresses she tells one child he can buy whatever he wants, but insists the second must spend her money on clothes. Later she tells the first to return some of what he purchased so he can buy clothes and school supplies. At the same time she takes most of the money away from the second child and gives it (and more) to the third. Not only this, but the third child, who up to now had no money at all, is allowed to buy whatever he wants! To your amazement this apparently capricious behavior goes on all day long.

Afterward you and your friend try to explain the mother's arbitrary behavior. Your friend assumes that everything was simply decided by the mother. After all, everything was in her power, so it's reasonable to assume she altered rules of spending at will. Unlike your friend, you have been acquainted with this woman and have always known her to be a kind, generous and very fair person. You therefore suspect that her arbitrariness was not due to her will alone. You insist that there must have been something else going on that you and your friend were not privy to.

To settle your disagreement you talk to the mother on the following day. It turns out you were right. You learn that the mother and her children had been involved in a rather elaborate game for a number of weeks. The mother had been trying to teach her three children about how the stock market operates, how fickle it can be and how to spend money responsibly in light of this. Without explaining any of the particulars of what transpired the day before, the mother outlined a few of the game's rules.

Each child originally had been assigned ten companies they would pretend to be shareholders in. The mother assigned values to the stock of each company; at the beginning of every day and on the hour throughout each day, each child was given or had to give back the money corresponding to the earnings or losses of their company. Moreover, to teach responsibility the mother had stipulated that earnings below a certain level had to be spent on necessities, like clothing, while earnings above a certain level could be spent on whatever the child pleased. However, if a particular stock fell and the child didn't have the money to cover the loss, he or she had to return the nonnecessary items purchased.

On trusting God. Though overly simplistic, I believe this analogy approximates the situation we find ourselves in. A drug addict who never wanted a child gives birth to a healthy baby while a godly woman conceives a longed-for child who dies at birth. One child is born into prosperity while another starves in poverty. One blind man is healed while others remain blind. One spouse escapes from a collapsing skyscraper while many others perish. One prayer is amazingly answered, but others seem to have no effect. God delivers the children of Israel out of Egypt, but not out of Auschwitz. Despite evidence of glorious design all around us, many times life feels like a roll of the dice.

Many people believe that since God has all power, the arbitrariness must be the result of his will. When five children are murdered by their mother, the father recites, "The Lord gives and the Lord takes." But Jesus suggested and Scripture intimates a far more complex scenario. Indeed, Job himself repented of this philosophy.

A wiser, more beneficial and Christ-centered approach is to suspect that something else is going on that we are not privy to. We know God in Jesus Christ, not just an aspect of God, a side of God, an attribute of God. *The fullness of the Godhead* was revealed in Christ (Col 2:9). He is the "exact imprint" of God's essence, his innermost heart (Heb 1:3). We thus can trust that God is perfect, self-sacrificial love (1 Jn 4:8). The cosmic arbitrariness that results in grotesque injustice, starving children and destroyed adults is not consistent with God's loving character and purpose. *Something else is going on.*

The trouble is, we can only guess at what else is going on. We can at best vaguely surmise some of the "rules of the game." And even when we surmise some of the rules (e.g., the necessary stability of the world and the irrevocability of freedom), we can't begin to know how they apply on a case by case basis.

This is what the book of Job is meant to communicate. Knowing that the world must be stable, that freedom must be irrevocable and that a vast, unknowable complexity engulfs every event in history helps us understand *in principle* why God cannot do more *in general*. But precisely because every event is engulfed in an unknowable complexity, we can never understand why God didn't do more in any particular circumstance.

Like the two observers in the above analogy, we only see the tail end of a long, complex and mostly unknown process. Indeed, we only see the last moves of an age-long "game" that is far more complex than we can begin to imagine. We experience the horror of a kidnapped child, for example, but have no clue about the immense network of factors behind it. Thus we can't begin to know why this person kidnapped this child at this moment, or why God couldn't intervene to stop it.

Given our myopic vision we can only fix our eyes on Jesus and trust that *God looks like him*. On this basis we trust that God's character and purposes are Calvary-like and thus that he is at all times doing everything possible to prevent evil. And when it isn't prevented, we trust him to bring good out it.

PRAYER AND AMBIGUITY

We have thus far discussed two variables that affect what God can and can't do in any given situation, given the kind of world he decided to create. The first is that the world in which agents relate must be regular, predictable and orderly. Thus God can't suspend the laws of nature whenever they might work against us. The second is that agents must possess irrevocable freedom. God simply can't override free wills whenever they might conflict with his will. Because God decided to create this kind of world, he can't ensure that his will is carried out in every situation. He must tolerate and wisely work around the irrevocable freedom of human and spirit agents.

When we combine these considerations with our awareness of the vast complexity of creation, we begin to understand how the world became a war zone and why we often experience life as arbitrary. We also begin to understand why God's interaction with us appears capricious despite the fact that in Christ we learn that God is not that way.

There is one more extremely important variable that conditions God's activity in any particular situation. It's especially important because it's a variable we can always do something about, which is perhaps why it's the one variable Jesus and the rest of Scripture emphasizes. I am speaking about prayer. Along with the necessary order of the world and the freedom of agents, Scripture consistently depicts prayer as significantly influencing God's interaction with us.

In this chapter I will discuss the power, rationale and principles of prayer. Understanding these will not only add to our appreciation of the unknowable complexity behind every event, but also help us understand our significant role in shaping what comes to pass. It will help motivate us to become people who pray.

THE POWER OF PRAYER

Does prayer really change things? Many pious people operating out of the blueprint model have said that the purpose of prayer is not to change God but to change us. From the blueprint perspective, how could they say anything different? If God is absolutely unchanging, and if everything that happens in the world is the unfolding of an eternal divine plan, there's nothing left for us to change.

Admittedly, prayer changes us and we certainly don't change God's character or his overall purpose for the world, but I suggest that the Bible presents a perspective very different than the blueprint worldview. Scripture encourages us to believe that prayer *really* changes what God does. Indeed, it sometimes changes *what God can do* in particular situations.

As with the first two variables we've discussed, this one isn't about God's power, for God is omnipotent. This variable is about the kind of world God decided to create. Scripture teaches that God created a world in which he has significantly bound himself to the prayers of his people.

The point is sprinkled throughout the biblical narrative. Consider Ezekiel 22:29-31. The Lord says:

> The people of the land have practiced extortion and committed robbery; they have oppressed the poor and needy, and have extorted from the alien without redress. And I sought for anyone among them who would repair the wall and stand in the breach before me on be-

half of the land, so that I would not destroy it; but I found no one. Therefore I have poured out my indignation upon them.

It's clear from this passage that God didn't want to judge his people, despite their unjust practices. Thus he sought for someone to prevent it. The Lord spoke as though there were a wall protecting his people from judgment, but the wall was being eroded by their sin. He sought someone to repair this wall and stand in the place where it was breaking so that judgment wouldn't come.

Most believe that "standing in the breach" refers to, or at least includes, intercessory prayer. After all, Scripture is full of examples of individuals and groups changing God's plan to judge people through intercessory prayer (e.g., Num 11:1-2; 14:12-20; 16:20-35; Deut 9:13-14, 18-20, 25; 2 Sam 24:17-25; 1 Kings 21:27-29; 2 Chron 12:5-8; Jer 26:19). To cite one specific example, David says:

> Therefore [the Lord] said he would destroy [the Israelites]—
>   had not Moses, his chosen one,
> stood in the breach before him,
>   to turn away his wrath from destroying them. (Ps 106:23)

The prayer of Moses changed God's plan (Ex 32:10-14). Unfortunately, in the situation we read about in Ezekiel, there was no intercessor like Moses to be found. And *this* is why judgment came upon Israel. We can't claim that prayer is beneficial without conceding that a lack of prayer is harmful.

We need to take this teaching very seriously. Note that the Lord doesn't say that prayer would have changed a person's *attitude* about God's judgment. The Lord says that prayer would have enabled God *to withhold judgment*. In light of this, it's difficult to avoid concluding that God has sovereignly designed the world such that prayer significantly influences him and the world.

Jesus on prayer. The above point was frequently emphasized by Jesus.

He taught us to pray that his Father's will would be done on earth as it is in heaven (Mt 6:10). The teaching only makes sense if God's will is *not* already being accomplished on earth. Moreover, it only makes sense if our prayer actually helps *bring about* God's will on earth. Prayer doesn't just change our attitude toward God's will: it *releases it* on the earth.

Along similar lines, Jesus repeatedly instructed us to ask God for things, promising us that they would be given (e.g., Mt 7:7, 11; 18:19-20; Jn 14:13-16; 15:7, 16; 16:23). Prayer doesn't just change our disposition about what we have or don't have. It affects what we have or don't have. Similarly, Jesus commanded us to pray with tireless persistence—*as though* God doesn't want to hear and answer our prayer (Lk 11:5-13; 18:1-8). This teaching assumes that the more we pray, the more good is accomplished, not just in us but in the world. Indeed, Jesus taught that prayer can move mountains. It doesn't simply change our attitudes toward mountains!

The Bible and prayer. There are more conditional promises attached to prayer in Scripture than to any other human activity.[1] *If* we pray, *then* God moves and the future is changed. For example, in an oft-quoted passage the Lord says:

> If my people who are called by my name humble themselves, pray, seek my face, and turn from their wicked ways, then I will hear from heaven, and will forgive their sin and heal their land. (2 Chron 7:14)

God wants to forgive. God wants to heal. But by God's own sovereign design, whether he gets what he wants in each particular instance is affected to some degree by whether or not his people humble themselves and pray.

John Wesley only slightly exaggerated the truth when he concluded that "God will do nothing but in answer to prayer."[2] The biblical narrative is shaped by God's response to prayer. From Cain's plea for leniency (Gen 4:13-15) to the Israelites' cry for liberation (Ex 2:23-25; 3:7-10;

Acts 7:34), from Moses' cry for help at the Red Sea and against the Amalakites (Ex 14:15-16; 17:8-14) to Hezekiah's prayer for an extension of life (2 Kings 20:1-7), and from Abraham's prayer for a son (Gen 15:2-6; 17:15-22; 21:1-3) to the leper's prayer for healing (Mt 8:2-3), the biblical narrative is woven together by examples of God moving in extraordinary ways in response to the prayers of his people.

James sums up the general teaching on prayer when he says that "the prayer of the righteous is powerful and effective" (Jas 5:16). It's powerful and effective not just in changing us but also in affecting God and therefore in changing the world.

THE RATIONALE FOR PRAYER

God conditions his supernatural involvement in the world in order to preserve the stability of the natural world and the integrity of free decisions. But why would God condition his involvement on the basis of prayer?

The need for God-human communication. God's primary objective is a world in which free agents love God and one another. For this to be possible, people need a stable environment and freely chosen, irrevocable, morally responsible say-so. Prayer is simply the spiritual side of our morally responsible say-so. We influence things by what we do through our bodies *and* in our communication with God.

More specifically, God's most important goal in creation is for humans to enter into a personal relationship with him. Relationships and communication are two sides of the same coin. We relate to others only as we communicate with them and they communicate with us. Hence, it makes sense for God to design a world that strongly encourages our communication with him. He conditions what he will do and what happens in the world on the basis of whether or not his people align their hearts with his in prayer. He designed the world so that a great deal of it revolves around and hinges on our communicating with him.

Prayer and morally responsible say-so. Prayer preserves our personhood in our relationship to God; a relationship in which one party is powerless is not a genuinely interpersonal relationship. Therefore God designed the world not only so *he will influence us* but also that *we might influence him.* This arrangement preserves our morally responsible freedom in relation to him. A significant degree of our say-so is connected to our communication with God. If we pray, things that should get done may get done. If we don't, these things will not get done. Just as the outcome of events genuinely hangs in the balance of our morally responsible decisions and behavior on a physical level, so too on a spiritual level. Our prayer really does make a difference!

We may think of prayer as the central way our God-intended place of authority is restored. Because God is relational and his central goal for creation is love, almost everything he does is through mediators. God's specific goal for humans from the start was to have us mediate his loving lordship over the earth. He created us to have dominion over the world (Gen 1:26-31). The New Testament declares that God wants a bride who will reign *with him* on earth (2 Tim 2:12; Rev 5:10; 20:6). For this reason, God gives us say-so not just on a physical level but also on a spiritual level. He empowers us to pray.

We may think of prayer as an essential aspect of our coreigning with God. He wants his will carried out on the earth, but he wants it carried out in cooperation with us. Thus to a significant degree, God's reign is applied on the earth only when we are coreigning with him by agreeing with him in prayer.

An illustration from Paul Billheimer is helpful. He says God's will is like a business check that must be cosigned in order to be validated. We the church are the cosigning party, and prayer is our signing.[3] Hence the essence of prayer is, as Jesus taught, to align our will with the Father's will so that his rule is established on earth as it is in heaven (Mt 6:10). In prayer we begin our eternal job of mediating the Father's will and reigning with Christ on earth.

The urgency of prayer. We must realize that if God is serious about our having morally responsible say-so on a spiritual level—coreigning with him—he must bind himself to the necessity of prayer, just as he binds himself to the stability of the world and to irrevocable freedom. God decided to create a world in which agents *really* have say-so on a spiritual level and *really* have the power to influence him and what comes to pass. Therefore things *really hang* on whether or not God's people pray. By his own design, prayer is a crucial variable that conditions what God can and can't do in any particular situation.

In contrast to the blueprint worldview, I believe that the warfare worldview I've been advocating in this book explains the remarkable urgency Scripture attaches to prayer. It also motivates us to pray more urgently. I have found that many people don't engage in passionate, persistent prayer simply because they have embraced a worldview in which prayer simply doesn't make sense. If God is going to do whatever he's going to do anyway, what's the point? These people may pray—they want to be obedient to the commands of Scripture—but so long as the effectiveness of prayer is inconsistent with their worldview, part of them will resist engaging in prayer as a matter of urgency. They engage in it more as a pro forma activity.

Urgency and finitude. As important as it is to stress the significance of our prayer, it's possible to go too far. We need a balanced perspective on prayer. After grasping the scriptural truth that things genuinely hang on prayer, some Christians wrongly conclude that almost everything hangs on prayer, even on their own personal prayer. Consequently they live in perpetual guilt for not praying enough, or perpetual anxiety over terrible things that may happen if they don't pray more. Conversely, others may be inclined toward spiritual grandiosity, concluding that magnificent things happen simply because they prayed. For example, I once encountered a man who claimed that communism ended in Russia because he "took authority over it in prayer"![4]

The need for balance in how we estimate our say-so on the spiritual level is in principle no different than on the physical level. We must neither ignore the responsibilities we do have nor live in condemnation over responsibilities we don't have. Healthy living is found in the balance between these two extremes. But this balance isn't always easy to maintain.

To illustrate, a number of years ago I participated in a missions trip to Haiti. I was overwhelmed by the depth of poverty I encountered in this country. Among other things, I was haunted by the memory of a young child looking for food in a pile of filthy garbage.

For the next year or so I lived in relentless guilt over every nonessential thing I enjoyed. I couldn't go to a movie, eat a nice meal, buy an ice cream cone or purchase new clothes without seeing this boy on top of the garbage pile. In torment I wondered, *What Haitian child will die today because I spent seven dollars on a movie?* The haunting condemnation destroyed my enjoyment of everything and almost paralyzed me. Moreover, because of my constant restlessness, it began to erode my marriage and friendships. It began to make me intensely bitter toward American culture and my own participation in it. Indeed, it was beginning to have a negative effect on my soul. Prolonged bitterness, for any reason, is never spiritually healthy.

The problem, I eventually came to realize, was that I had lost my balance. It was of course a good thing that the plight of the boy jarred my lifestyle and called into question my Western values. It was a good thing for me to take some responsibility for the poor and to question how I was using my economic say-so as an American to combat this problem. Lord knows most Western Christians need to be jarred like this and to take more responsibility! But the emotive force of this image caused me to forget my finitude. I had reduced the vast complexity of the world to a simple zero-sum game in which everything I enjoyed was at someone else's expense. Without going into the complex issues surrounding global economic justice, suffice it to say that my perspective was overly simplistic, short-sighted and unproductive.

The reality of the situation is that I was clearly called by God to take responsibility for *some* children in Haiti and to sacrificially make a difference in their lives. But I could only do this effectively when I acknowledged that I am not responsible for *every* child in Haiti. I learned that I was to take responsibility for that which God made me responsible and let him take ultimate responsibility for everything else. More specifically, I realized that while I couldn't feed and house all the children in Haiti, I could help feed and house, say, a dozen. And I came to realize that when I long to do my Father's will, I must be content making the difference he calls and empowers me to.

While there are principles of justice we can and must live by, there is no ironclad ethical rule that stipulates in any particular instance how much or little a given person is responsible for. Living a healthy, balanced kingdom life in an ambiguous war zone is not a matter of following a set of rules but of faithfully following God's leading. Every person's situation and calling is different. We simply have to lay our lives before God and in all honesty seek his will. We have to realize that though things genuinely hang on how we use our say-so, our say-so is finite.

Finding balance in our prayer life is no different. Since we can spend only so much time in intercessory prayer, and since there is virtually an infinite number of things we could pray for, praying for direction on how we should spend our say-so in prayer is extremely important. As with our economic say-so, our prayer life has to avoid the Scylla of thinking that *nothing* genuinely hangs on our prayer and the Charybdis of assuming that *everything* hangs on our prayer.

Why is prayer unanswered? Understanding prayer as our spiritual say-so helps us understand why God conditions his activity on the basis of our prayer. This explains why prayer is a matter of urgency. It also explains why God's responses to prayer often seem so arbitrary. On the authority of Scripture we must believe that all prayer is "powerful and effective" in changing the world (Jas 5:16). But obviously not all prayer brings about what we are praying for. So the natural question is, why is one prayer answered while another is not?

In the blueprint worldview the ultimate answer to this question could only be that God didn't will to answer the second prayer. However mysterious it may seem, we must believe there is a divine reason for everything—including unanswered prayer. My understanding of prayer provides a different explanation.

The arbitrary way prayer seems to be answered is not primarily a function of God's mysterious will, though God's will is an important factor to consider in thinking about this question. In the end this is unanswerable for the same reason that questions about why particular things happen the way they do are unanswerable. We pray and God responds in the context of an unfathomably complex creation that is racked by cosmic war.

On the authority of Jesus Christ and the biblical witness we can be assured that prayer *always* furthers God's purpose in the world. Yet prayer is not the only variable that influences what God can and can't do in any particular situation within this complex war zone. Among other things, God must respect the necessary stability of the world and the irrevocable freedom of vast multitudes of free agents. Prayer makes a difference, but so do the necessary regularity of the world and every free choice humans and angels make. We have no way of knowing how the power of prayer intersects with these and other variables.

We can pray with confidence, knowing our prayer is heard and makes a difference. But we can't pray with certainty that the difference our prayer makes will have the precise outcome we desire. In this sense we can't be certain our prayer will be answered.

This is in principle no different than the fact that we know our morally responsible actions on a physical level have a long term impact, though we usually can't know precisely what this impact will be. The difference, of course, is that the impact of our prayer is usually less visible to us than our physical actions—even though the actual impact of our prayer may be much greater. This is why it takes persistent faith to be a person of prayer, as Jesus taught us.

VARIABLES RELATED TO PRAYER

There is another rarely noticed but extremely important reason why we often can't know why prayer is or isn't answered. While prayer itself is as simple as talking to a friend, the actual mechanics of prayer are remarkably complex. Scripture hints at a number of variables that affect the impact prayer has on the world.

In what follows I will briefly review nine variables alluded to in Scripture that affect the outcome of prayer. Each of these is, in its own way, a variable that may affect what God does in a particular situation. We may think of them as analogous to the laws of nature that allow agents to relate to each other. Just as God designed our physical environment to have regular rules that allow us to have say-so on a physical level, so God designed our spiritual environment to have regular rules that allow us to have say-so on a spiritual level.

These rules are variables that structure and condition the power of our prayer. They are important for us to review for two reasons: (1) so we can pray with as much effectiveness as possible, and (2) so we further appreciate that we can't ordinarily know why any given prayer is or is not answered. More specifically, our awareness of the complex mechanics of prayer helps us locate the mystery of unanswered prayer in the unknowable complexity of creation rather than in the will of God.

1. God's will. I have argued against appealing to God's will as the *only* explanation for why prayer is or isn't answered. Yet God's will is the most basic variable affecting whether prayer is answered. John says we should be bold in prayer, having confidence that if we ask anything *according to his will*, he hears us (1 Jn 5:14). And James teaches us that we don't receive what we request because we are asking with selfish motives, not considering God's will for our life (Jas 4:3).

Similarly, Jesus' request for the Father to find a plan other than the cross couldn't be granted because it wasn't the Father's will. Thus Jesus concluded, "yet not what I want but what you want" (Mt 26:39). So too

Paul's request that his thorn in the flesh be removed was not granted, for the Lord saw that he could use Paul more with this thorn than without it (2 Cor 12:7-10).

Clearly, praying in accordance with God's will is a crucial variable in determining the outcome. It's important, however, for us to see that in the case of Jesus, "God's will" was not necessarily God's *ideal* will. It was rather God's will *accommodated* to the situation of a fallen world. Jesus' death grieved the Father, but it simply wasn't possible to save the world in any other fashion. The Father willed the death of his Son in the sense that he willed the reconciliation of the world *more* than he willed sparing his own Son. And Jesus willed to carry out his Father's accommodating will more than he willed avoiding the physical, mental and spiritual torture he was about to endure.

Something similar is true in the case of Paul. It was Satan, not God, who originally gave Paul his thorn in the flesh. But even though Jesus uniformly expressed God's will as being against sickness and disease, *in this case* Jesus saw that it was more beneficial to leave the infirmity in place. Indeed, Paul suggests that *in this case* Satan was specifically allowed to torment him for this very reason (2 Cor 12:7). It wasn't God's ideal will to have Paul afflicted, but given Paul's struggle with pride, allowing him to be afflicted was closer to God's ideal than removing it. In cases such as these, therefore, we might say that God's will is his awareness of the greatest good achievable in a nonideal situation.

We must be careful not to conclude that because God willed something, it is part of "his perfect plan." Even with this qualification, however, we must be even more careful not to generalize Jesus' or Paul's experience to the point of concluding that *every* instance of suffering and every unanswered prayer are part of God's accommodating will. There are a number of variables influencing the outcome of prayer. Moreover, as discussed in a previous chapter, there are variables that condition God's response to prayer, and these have nothing directly to do with prayer or God's specific will in a given situation.

2. The faith of the person being prayed for. Everywhere Jesus went, multitudes of people were healed and delivered, except in his own hometown. Mark explains why: "he could do no deed of power there, except that he laid his hands on a few sick people and cured them. And he was amazed at their unbelief "(Mk 6:5-6). He couldn't do any deeds of power there! Jesus *wanted* to heal and deliver people in his hometown as much as anywhere else. But in this case Jesus couldn't do what he wanted because the people lacked faith.

This passage teaches us that the faith of a person being prayed for is a variable in determining whether or not the prayer is answered. The principle was expressed throughout Jesus' ministry. Many times, after healing a person Jesus went so far as to say "your faith has made you well" (Mt 9:22; cf. Lk 7:50; 17:19).

Here too a word of caution is in order. Some, recognizing that God's ideal will is to heal people, have concluded that whenever someone is not healed or a prayer is not answered it's because the person being prayed for lacked faith.[5] We must not generalize to the point of making this principle *the* explanation for why prayer is or isn't answered. This is as misguided as making God's will *the* explanation for why prayer is or isn't answered. At the same time, we need to be aware that the faith of the person(s) being prayed for is *a* variable that sometimes influences prayer.

3. The faith of people praying for others. Many times in the ministry of Jesus the effectiveness of prayer was associated with the faith of the people praying for others, not the faith of those being prayed for. For example, when a group of people took the trouble to dismantle a roof and lower a paralyzed friend into an overcrowded room so Jesus could heal him, Luke says that Jesus "saw their faith" and thus healed their friend (Lk 5:20). Similarly, when a centurion asked Jesus to heal his servant, Jesus responded by saying, "Go; let it be done for you according to your faith" (Mt 8:13). His servant was immediately healed. Yet nothing was said about the faith of this servant.

On the negative side, Jesus implied that one reason his disciples were unable to cast a demon out of a boy was because they lacked faith (Mk 9:14-19), though he later also stressed other variables that hindered the disciples in this instance. But the faith of the demonized boy was not relevant. Indeed, the same is true in every deliverance account we have in the Gospels.

The principle here is that the strength of our faith in praying for another person increases the power of our prayer. James taught that we must "ask in faith, never doubting, for the one who doubts is like a wave of the sea, driven and tossed by the wind; for the doubter, being double-minded and unstable in every way, must not expect to receive anything from the Lord" (Jas 1:6-7).

Again, we must avoid reducing this principle to a simplistic formula that explains all instances of unanswered prayer. Whenever we turn principles into formulas, we end up either indicting God or other people. Reality is always more complex than our formulas. But the *principle* holds true: our faith, the faith of the person we're praying for and God's knowledge of what is possible and advantageous in a given situation affect whether our prayer will have the outcome we are praying for.

4. Persistence of prayer. A fourth factor in the outcome of prayer is our persistence. We have no reason to think that spiritual work is all that different than physical work, and we know that physical work often takes persistence. Some rocks can be lifted in a minute, but others take hours. So it is in prayer.

Jesus taught that when we pray we should be like the woman who persistently knocked on her neighbor's door to get some food for a guest (Lk 11:5-8). Jesus concludes this analogy with his famous teaching, "Ask, and it will be given you; search, and you will find; knock, and the door will be opened for you" (v. 9). In this context it's clear that asking, searching and knocking are persistent, laboring prayer. Prayer is not magic; it is spiritual labor.

In another parable Jesus spoke about our "need to pray always and not to lose heart" (Lk 18:1). He said we should pray like a woman trying to get her case settled by an unjust and reluctant judge. Jesus concluded by asking, "When the Son of Man comes, will he find faith on earth?" (Lk 18:1-8). This parable is about prayer, not the nature of God. (It's not implying that God is like an unjust judge; prayer is not a matter of twisting God's arm.) Jesus' point is simply that we should pray—with persistence—like people who desperately need something. Clearly Jesus taught that to pray with faith is to pray without losing heart. We should, in the words of Paul, "pray without ceasing" (1 Thess 5:17).

Again, we must be careful to avoid simplistic, formulaic overgeneralizations. Jesus' teaching on the need for persistence doesn't mean that whenever a prayer isn't answered it's because we didn't pray long enough. There are, we are learning, a multitude of factors that influence the outcome of prayer. It does mean, though, that when a matter of prayer is on our heart, we should be persistent about it. And for all we know, *in some cases* our persistence may be the decisive variable in determining whether our prayer is answered.

5. *The number of people praying.* When dealing with an important matter, most people of faith instinctively ask others to pray with them. The assumption is that with more people praying, it's more likely that this matter will be resolved in accordance with the prayer. This assumption is reasonable. For as we noted above, principles that ordinarily apply on our earthly level usually also apply on a spiritual level.

We all know that some physical and mental tasks can be accomplished alone but others require help. The bigger the rock, the more likely it is you'll need help lifting it. There is no reason to think that the labor of prayer is any different. Scripture, experience and even several scientific studies support the conclusion that prayer is not at all different than physical or mental work in this regard.[6]

We see this principle being acted on in Scripture when large groups of people were called together to pray or when biblical characters ask others to join them in prayer (e.g., Neh 9:1; 2 Chron 7:14; Mt 26:36, 41; Acts 1:13-14; 4:24-30; Eph 6:19-20; Col 4:3-4; 1 Thess 5:25; 2 Thess 3:1; Heb 13:18; Jas 5:13-16). We also find this principle endorsed by Jesus when he taught, "If two of you agree on earth about anything you ask, it will be done for you by my Father in heaven. For where two or three are gathered in my name, I am there among them" (Mt 18:19-20). The teaching assumes that there is an additional dimension of power available when others agree with you in making a request. Indeed, there is a dimension of Christ's presence when we pray with others that is absent when we pray alone.

This, of course, is not to say that solitary prayer is vacuous or that Christ is not present when a person prays alone. Nor does the passage mean that if two people agree about a matter of prayer, the answer is guaranteed. To be sure, Jesus expressed this teaching in unqualified terms: "It will be done for you." But he and other biblical teachers sometimes spoke the same way about individual prayer (e.g., Mt 21:22; Mk 11:24; Jn 14:13-14; 15:7, 16). We should take the unqualified language as hyperbole, that is, exaggeration for the purpose of emphasis. This manner of speech was common among Jews of the time and is found throughout the Bible (e.g., Ps 37:25; Prov 22:6; Mk 9:47). Emphatic, unqualified language sometimes functioned for them the way an exclamation mark functions in our language; it was a way of stressing a point.

In any event, taking these passages literally brings them into conflict with other biblical passages about the outcome of prayer, as we are seeing. Moreover, they conflict with universal human experience, for no individual or group always has prayers answered exactly as requested. Nevertheless, the principle that there is power in numbers has to be factored into our understanding of the outcome of prayer.

6. Human free will. A sixth variable to take into account is the free will of the people we are praying for. For example, we may pray for someone's salvation, and this will undoubtedly increase the influence of the Holy Spirit in his or her life. But God will not—and given the kind of world he has created, *cannot*—simply override a person's free will to answer our prayer. Indeed, if God could simply override the free will of people to get them saved, we have every reason to believe *everyone would be saved* (see 1 Tim 2:4-6, 4:10; 2 Pet 3:9)! Hell is a testimony to how seriously God takes free will. Yet God designed the world such that prayer affects him and conditions his influence in the world, so we can be confident that praying for a person's salvation increases the Spirit's influence on that person.

Similarly, we should pray for protection when we drive, and this will render it more likely that we won't be harmed. Still, so long as other drivers can make morally responsible (or irresponsible) choices that affect others, our complete safety can't be guaranteed. Prayer affects everything, but it may not have the outcome we are praying for; it is persuasive, not coercive. People still make free choices.

This view of prayer will strike some people as strange. They are unaccustomed to thinking of divine power as *influence*. Perhaps under the impact of the blueprint worldview they think about divine power strictly in terms of control. Yet the kind of power we are most familiar with is influence, not control. For example, I am trying to influence your thinking about prayer right now, but I cannot (and do not desire to) *control* you.

In a similar fashion God works primarily by influencing us at the level of our innermost being. By his own design his influence in a person's life is intensified when his people pray for that person. This is part of our morally responsible say-so. Yet, also by his own design, he will not undermine a person's say-so by controlling him or her, regardless of how much we pray. It's urgent that we pray for people's hearts, whether for their salvation or, say, for their waning love for their spouse. And we can have confidence that this prayer, like all prayer, increases God's influence. But God will not—and by his own self-limitation cannot—simply turn people into robots to answer our prayer.

7. *Angelic free will.* Human beings are not the only agents in the cosmos who possess morally responsible say-so. Spirit agents (referred to in Scripture as angels, gods, demons, principalities, powers, authorities, rulers) also possess free will. Their activity is another variable that influences prayer.

In chapter four we discussed the case of Daniel. When Daniel began praying and fasting, God immediately dispatched an angel in response to his prayer. Yet the answer to Daniel's prayer was delayed twenty-one days because the angel was resisted by "the prince of Persia" (Dan 10:12-13). Though we Western people rarely if ever consider spiritual warfare a factor in determining the outcome of our prayers, this episode alone is enough to teach us otherwise. Often when prayers (or plans) don't bring about the outcome we hoped, people say something like "God's timing is the right timing." But this is too simplistic. The delay Daniel experienced had nothing to do with God's timing but with interference in the spiritual realm.

Similarly, Paul writes to the Thessalonians that he had "great eagerness to see you face to face. For we wanted to come to you—certainly I, Paul, wanted to again and again." Yet, unfortunately, this didn't happen because "Satan blocked our way" (1 Thess 2:17-18). Paul doesn't mention whether or not he prayed to be able to see the Thessalonians, but it's hard to imagine that he didn't. In any event the passage teaches us that spirit agents' decisions and activities intersect with ours.

At the very least this passage reveals that neither God's will nor our eagerness and faith—or any other variable we might appeal to—stands alone as *the* determinative variable of what comes to pass. Spirit agents affect what we do and what God does, including how he responds to our prayer.

Walter Wink notes that at least in some circumstances "Principalities and Powers are able to hold [the Lord] at bay."[7] From this he concludes that "prayer involves not just God and people, but God and people and the Powers. What God is able to do in the world is hindered, to a considerable extent, by the rebelliousness, resistance, and self-interest of the Powers exercising their freedom under God."[8]

When we ignore this important variable, we oversimplify matters and often end up "blaming God for evils committed by the Powers." In contrast to this, Wink says, "prayer that acknowledges the Powers becomes a form of social action."[9] All prayer that furthers God's will on earth confronts spiritual powers that resist God's will from being accomplished on earth.

8. The number and strength of spirit agents. There is another variable in the role that spirit agents play in affecting the outcome of our prayer. In the physical world we have no trouble accepting that the number of the forces on either side of a battle is a significant factor in deciding its outcome. Yet we Westerners customarily ignore this piece of common sense when it comes to thinking about spiritual warfare. We forget that things in the spiritual realm are not dissimilar to things in the physical realm. The Bible never divorces these two realms in this fashion.

In Daniel's case, note that the angel battling "the prince of Persia" was freed to come to Daniel because "Michael, one of the chief princes, came to help me" (Dan 10:13). Not only this, but the angel told Daniel he had to leave quickly and "return to fight against the prince of Persia" (Dan 10:20). The passage clearly assumes that the strength and number of angels fighting on one side or the other made a difference in what transpired.

If Michael or some other agent in God's court (e.g., Job 1:6; 2:1; Ps 82; 89:7; Jer 23:18, 22) hadn't been available to help this messenger, it would have taken even longer for Daniel to hear a response to his prayer.[10] Even though Michael is "one of the chief princes," he needed help in fighting the "prince of Persia." Thus the angel delivering the message had to leave quickly. What goes on in the spiritual realm is influenced by the strength and number of spirit agents who are fighting, and the outcome of these battles can affect God's response to our prayer. If our will can fulfill or thwart God's purposes for our life and those we influence, why should we think matters are different with angels?

Throughout Scripture, battles that rage in the spiritual realm are depicted the same way as battles in the physical realm. And Scripture assumes these two realms influence each other. For example, when Elisha's servant worried that they were surrounded by foes, Elisha told him, "Do not be afraid, for there are more with us than there are with them." He then prayed for his servant's eyes to be opened, at which point the servant saw that they were surrounded by a vast army of heavenly hosts (2 Kings 6:16-17).

When facing the Philistines in battle, David was told to move his troops to a particular place and wait till he heard "the sound of marching in the tops of the balsam trees." This would show him that "the LORD has gone out before you to strike down the army of the Philistines" (2 Sam 5:24). Earthly and heavenly battles intersect with one another, and on both levels the outcome of the battle is connected to the strength and numbers on both sides.

We see hints of the significance of this variable in Jesus' ministry. Jesus once confronted a powerful, demonized person who could not be restrained even with "shackles and chains" (Mk 5:1-4). Jesus commanded the spirit to "come out of the man," but the demon didn't respond immediately (Mk 5:7-8). Jesus then asked, "What is your name?" and the demon identified himself as "Legion, for we are many" (Mk 5:9).

It's not too difficult to conclude that the reason the demons were able to resist Jesus' initial command was precisely because there were so many of them, and like a Roman legion, they were united in purpose. Perhaps because of the resistance he encountered, Jesus asked for a name, which he didn't do at any other point in his ministry. In ancient Jewish culture a being's name was associated with its character and mission. Thus it's reasonable to conclude that Jesus was investigating the source of strength he was confronting in this man.

In Mark 9 we discover that the strength and "kind" of spirit agent involved in a battle also influences what comes to pass. Here we find Jesus confronting a young boy who was powerfully demonized. The boy was mute, violent and suicidal (Mk 9:17-18, 22). Though his disciples had performed a number of successful exorcisms before this time, they had been unsuccessful in casting out this one. When they asked Jesus why this was so, he replied, "*This kind* can come out only through prayer" (vv. 28-29, italics added). It seems evident that there are different kinds of demons with varying degrees of strength, and extraordinary spiritual labor is needed to overcome these "strong ones."

One further illustration: following a dispute about how Jesus cast out demons (Lk 11:14-20) Jesus taught his disciples, "When a strong man, fully armed, guards his castle, his property is safe. But when one stronger than he attacks him and overpowers him, he takes away his armor in which he trusted and divides his plunder" (Lk 11:22-23). Jesus was referring to Satan as a "strong man" and himself as "one stronger than he," but the principle behind the teaching may be generalized. The relative strength of opposing forces in a spiritual battle factors into the outcome of the battle. Only one stronger than the strong man can overcome him.

As Jesus continued his teaching, he touched on the significance of the number of opposition forces. If a person who has had "an unclean spirit" cast out isn't careful, the spirit may eventually return with "seven spirits more evil than itself" and take up residence in the person once again. In this case "the last state of that person is worse than the first" (Lk 11:24-26). Again we see that the greater the number of spirit agents we are up against, the worse the situation we're in. Yet Christians should not fear, because we know that the Spirit of Christ in us is greater than the spirit that is in the world (1 Jn 4:4).

At the same time, this principle helps us understand why we can't know whether or not a given prayer will be answered. That outcome may be influenced by the number of forces resisting or aligned with our prayer. But unless God gifts a person with "the discernment of spirits" (1 Cor 12:10), we have no way of knowing about these spiritual battles. This should caution us against simplistic theologies that claim to know more than we can know by reducing the complexity and ambiguity of life to one or two formulaic variables.

9. The presence of sin. After suffering a terrible defeat, Joshua and the elders of Israel fell on their faces in prayer to God. But the Lord said to Joshua, "Stand up! Why have you fallen upon your face? Israel has sinned" (Josh 7:10-11). What was required in this situation was not prayer but confronting sin. This episode illustrates the principle that in some cases God wants us to do something (e.g., repent or confront sin) before he will hear our prayer. For example, no one would be surprised if God told an abusive husband that prayer for his wife's love is useless until he stops abusing her!

Scripture generally teaches that the presence of known sin in a person's life hinders the power of his or her prayer. For example, Jesus taught his disciples to make sure they have forgiven everybody before they pray (Mk 11:25). James specifically connects confession with the power of prayer in bringing healing to a person. He concludes that it is "the prayer *of the righteous*" that is "powerful and effective" (Jas 5:16, italics added).

Similarly, one of the reasons Peter commands husbands to honor their wives is "so that nothing may hinder your prayers" (1 Pet 3:7). Sinning against your spouse affects your ability to communicate effectively with God. The Psalmist taught that the Lord would not listen to those who cherish iniquity in their hearts (Ps 66:18). And the author of Proverbs taught that when no consideration is given to God's law, "even one's prayers are an abomination" (Prov 28:9). Like a clog in the faucet, sin blocks the flow of God's power in our prayer life.

Of course we must avoid the dreadful conclusion that the prayer of people with sin is useless, for we are all sinners (especially the one who claims to have no sin, 1 Jn 1:10)! Therefore we must not assume that a prayer wasn't answered because of sin in a person's life. Except in obvious cases—for example, an abusive husband's prayer for his wife to love him—only God can know this.

Nevertheless, it's important to know that the spiritual condition of the person praying is one variable affecting his or her prayer life.

PRAYER AND THE IMPENETRABLE AMBIGUITY OF LIFE

This list of nine variables affecting prayer isn't exhaustive. Indeed, Scripture hints at other variables that may influence the power of prayer. For example, fasting and laying on of hands during prayer appear frequently in Scripture. Nevertheless, the nine variables sufficiently demonstrate that as simple as prayer is, its mechanics are rather complex.

Knowing what you can't know. Understanding these variables helps us pray more effectively. But it also helps us know how little we know. As in many other areas, the more we learn about reality, the more we become aware of how much we don't know about it. Indeed, the more we know, the more we discover our essential finitude, that is, what we *can't* know. As an increasing number of scientists are acknowledging, the more we confront the incredible complexity and intricate design of creation, the more profoundly we are humbled.[11]

So it is with theology in general and the mechanics of prayer in particular. The more we learn about the God-designed rules that govern our communication with him, and the more we consider other variables that condition what God does in his creation, the more we realize how precious little we can know about the particulars of God's interaction with us. The very process of learning the principles by which God interacts with us reveals the impossibility of knowing how these principles interact with each other. We are humbled in the face of our ignorance about the complexity of the creation.

This humble acceptance of finitude is very beneficial. If followed through in faith, it helps us relinquish our fear of ambiguity (see chapter one) and our inclination to oversimplify creation and overcomplicate God's character and purposes (which have been unambiguously revealed in Christ). It also helps us to more fully appreciate that the mystery of evil is not a mystery about God but about creation. Finally, it thus helps us to completely trust in Christ, who is the full revelation of God.

A case study in what we can and can't know. Several years ago a married couple I know and love was involved in a tragic car accident that resulted in the death of their thirteen-year-old son. Understandably, the accident raised a number of tormenting questions for them. Among other things, they wondered what role God or Satan may have played in this accident. If anyone was to die, they wondered, why not one of them instead of their son? And what perhaps tormented them most of all, they wondered if their son's death was in any way their own fault. Was their son killed because they had allowed him to take off his seat belt to play a game in the back seat of their car? Or was it that they hadn't prayed enough for protection?

Many Christians would resolve the ambiguity these questions create by appealing to God's will. There is a divine reason for everything, so we must trust that God willed this accident for a good reason. Unfortunately, others might venture further, as Melanie's instructor did, in an attempt to offer insight into what God's purpose actually was. Perhaps God was teaching the parents (or somebody else) a lesson. For my part, the wisest response to these kinds of questions is to emphasize how much we know about God in Jesus Christ, and how little we know about the complex world.

We know that God is decisively revealed in Jesus Christ, and thus we may assume that whatever isn't consistent with the character of Christ was not his doing. If this accident could have been supernaturally prevented, we have every reason to assume God would have prevented it. Remember, Jesus asked, "Father, *if it is possible* . . ." To know in any detail why it was not possible, however, we'd have to be omniscient. We'd have to have complete knowledge of all the variables that affect God's interaction with us as well as how each of these variables has played out in every event in the history of the cosmos.

To answer the questions this couple raised, we would have to know everything about

1. the necessary regularity of the laws of nature
2. the irrevocable freedom God has granted to every human and angelic agent ever created
3. how these decisions intersected with one another and influenced subsequent events
4. the variables that regulate prayer
5. how these variables played out not only in the prayers of this family but in the prayers of everyone who prayed for this family

All these are aspects of the mystery of God's unfathomably complex creation. And these are matters we can't—or at least shouldn't—even begin to guess at. When we reduce principles to formulas and our world of ambiguity and complexity to the will of God (or the faith of the couple), nothing but harm results. God's character is tarnished and people are wounded. We have to know what we can know—God's character and purpose revealed in Christ—and what we can't know—the mystery of creation.

Praying in a sea of ambiguity. If the couple involved in the car accident had prayed more for protection, would their accident have been avoided? This is as unanswerable as the question of whether a seat belt would have saved the child's life. Perhaps, but we can't know. After all, thousands of people who wear seat belts die in car accidents each year. We could just as pointlessly speculate about whether the accident would have been avoided if the weather had been different, if the family would have slept in (putting them on the road at a different time) or if a butterfly hadn't flapped its wings in a certain manner last month in Argentina. There is an almost infinite set of contingencies leading up to every event. But there is nothing we can do about them and nothing to be gained by speculating about such matters.

This includes the role that prayer did or didn't have in this accident. To be sure, we can know that praying always makes a difference. (For all we know, the prayer of this family may have been a decisive factor in preventing others from being killed in this accident.) The difference prayer makes is associated with what God knows is possible and beneficial in a particular situation. It's also associated with the faith of the person praying as well that of the people being prayed for. The persistence, number and character of the people praying are also factors.

But prayer is also conditioned by the free decisions people make— like the woman who inadvertently cut the family off on the highway— by the free decisions of spirit agents, by the strength and numbers of spiritual forces aligning themselves with or against the prayer, and by the regularity of the laws of nature. To answer the couple's question about whether prayer could have spared their son, we would have to know everything about all these variables: *we'd have to be omniscient.*

Who can say what God knew was possible in this situation? Or do we know the degree of faith this couple had or the faith of those who might have prayed for them? Would anyone claim to know whether greater persistence or a greater number of people praying would have changed the outcome of this tragic trip?

Who knows whether the impact of all free decisions ever made throughout history would not have overridden more prayer? Can anyone claim to know whether or not spiritual forces were involved in this accident, or in any other event that might have influenced this accident? Does anyone claim to know how many agents were working in one direction or another, and how much say-so each agent possessed?

Conclusion

The answer to all these questions, of course, is a resounding no. We know next to nothing about any of this. We pray as we live: in a sea of ambiguity. This is not because we are fallen but because we are finite. And we are inclined to forget we are finite. We ignore the ambiguity that accompanies our finitude, and thus we claim to know what we can't know. We reduce the unfathomable complexity of the cosmos to the capacity of our finite minds. When we do this, we invariably end up blaming God or indicting victims. We align ourselves with Job's ignorant and arrogant friends, with whom God was very angry (Job 42:7).

We pray best, live best and counsel best when we keep our eyes fixed on the God we know in Jesus Christ, remembering the sea of ambiguity that surrounds every square inch of this precious knowledge.

SEVEN

LIFE AND HOPE

The mystery of evil isn't about God's character or purposes but about the incomprehensible complexity of a cosmos engulfed in spiritual war. The reason the events of life, including God's response to prayer, seem so arbitrary is that we know next to nothing about the vast network of influences shaping every event.

For this reason, the mystery of why a particular evil afflicts a particular person is in principle no different than the mystery that surrounds every contingent event. To fully understand anything—for example, why a hurricane formed when and where it did, why one person won the lottery instead of another, why a particular duck landed on a particular pond at a particular time—we'd have to ultimately know every variable in world history. If anything had been different, the world now would have been slightly—or even significantly—different, and the event might not have occurred just as it did.

Understanding our freedom and finitude helps us comprehend how evil *can* happen in God's creation and why we usually *can't* penetrate the mystery of why things happen as they do. However, understanding this *doesn't* help us live in the midst of this war-torn sea of ambiguity. So the question we must now ask is, How can we effectively live in this sea of ambiguity? And how are we to find solace, hope and courage in this situation, especially when we or someone we love becomes a casualty of war?

While every situation is a little different and thus formulaic answers must be avoided, I will offer six biblically based principles that can help us live passionately and cope effectively in this war-torn sea of ambiguity.

PRINCIPLE 1: FIX YOUR EYES UPON JESUS

The book of Hebrews addresses Christians facing possible persecution for their faith. Like Jesus, they knew that they might have to suffer or even die for their allegiance to God. Using the analogy of an endurance race, the author encourages them, and us, to "run with perseverance the race that is set before us, looking to Jesus, the pioneer and perfecter of our faith" (Heb 12:1-2).

Throughout our endurance race, our eyes must be fixed on Jesus. We won't have the fortitude to complete this often grueling endeavor without him. The love Jesus expressed in dying for us motivates us. The example he set in dying to bring about the kingdom of God inspires us. And perhaps most important, the truth of what God is like, which Jesus revealed throughout his life and death, reassures us. Christian faith is trusting that no matter how things go in life, God's stance toward us is the same as Jesus'. He loves us with an unwavering, unsurpassable, self-sacrificial love.

One of the greatest mistakes people make is assuming they can draw conclusions about the nature of God from life's experiences. Allowing everyday events to influence their picture of God causes some to mistrust or harbor resentment against him. It leads others to become atheists and accounts for much of the apathy sincere Christians feel toward God. As with Melanie, when our picture of God is influenced by the tragic events of life, it's difficult to be passionate about him.

When our eyes are fixed on Jesus, however, and when we understand that the seemingly arbitrary vicissitudes of life reflect the war-torn nature of the cosmos, but not the character of God, our hearts are aroused with passionate love for him. Indeed, the apostle Paul taught us that the primary way we are transformed "from one degree of glory to another" is by gazing on "the glory of God in the face of Jesus Christ" (2 Cor 3:18; 4:6). As we become increasingly enraptured by God's beauty revealed in Jesus, we are transformed—despite the misfortune we may have faced. But when we let *our experience* define the Father, we are deformed by apathy, confusion and perhaps even unbelief.

Fixing our eyes on Jesus also transforms our understanding of God's attitude toward evil. The fact that Christ suffered a godforsaken death on Calvary shows us that God is willing to experience judgment and death to bring evil to an end. God is not a heavenly spectator looking down on human misery. Nor is he a secret accomplice behind evil activity, though he is always at work to use evil to his and our advantage. Short of abandoning his plan to allow people to freely love him, God has done and is still doing everything possible to remove evil from his creation. And we are assured of his ultimate victory.

Calvary is God's ultimate answer to the problem of evil. If anyone suffers because of the risky nature of the cosmos, it is *God*. And his suffering, combined with his work in and through the church, is what defeats the devil and ultimately transforms the world (1 Jn 3:8; Heb 2:14).

Principle 2: Remember That God Is with You

Jesus knew his disciples would suffer because of their commitment to follow him. In fact, while many people today wonder why "bad things happen to good people," the New Testament teaches that "good people" should *expect* to suffer (Jn 16:33; 1 Thess 3:4). The world is, after all, a war zone. To console his disciples, Jesus told them, "Remember, I am with you always, to the end of the age" (Mt 28:20).

When people go through radical suffering, they often feel alone. After all, how many others can relate to losing a baby in childbirth, a spouse in a terrorist attack or a loved one to leukemia? This sense of aloneness greatly intensifies the pain. Support groups formed by those who have endured similar tragedies are healing for this very reason: the participants realize that they're really not alone in their suffering.

Those who place their trust in Jesus Christ need never feel alone, regardless of the tremendous emotional or physical pain they are enduring. God is with them. Unfortunately, many who assume God is in meticulous control of every event angrily push him away just when they need him the most! It's vitally important that in the midst of suffering we remember *God is with us and is on our side.* Indeed, the New Testament teaches that our suffering is a participation in Christ's suffering. We suffer with him (Rom 8:17; Col 1:24). The cross reveals not just what God did for us once but God's love for us always. God is with us sharing in our experience, suffering with our suffering.

Even if you believed no other human on earth could understand your grief, God understands and shares in it (Heb 4:15-16). Remembering this increases our love for God and gives us strength to go on. In fact, though it's difficult to believe sometimes, God's abiding presence in our life can give us a profound peace—God's own peace—in any situation (Jn 14:27). In the words of Paul, it is "the peace of God, which surpasses all understanding" (Phil 4:7). This peace is not based on the circumstances of life, which is why it "surpasses all undersanding." It comes from having a relationship with Christ, who is living in you and sharing in all you go through. It's nothing less than the perfect peace of the eternal Trinity, who is never caught off guard, never anxious and never overwhelmed. Though he has designed a world in which he experiences frustration, grief and anger, God remains supremely tranquil and confident. And he wants to share this eternally tranquil confidence with all who will open themselves up to him.

PRINCIPLE 3: YIELD TO HIS GRACIOUS REDEMPTIVE POWER

After talking about the suffering that permeates creation (Rom 8:19-27), Paul reassures believers by giving them this wonderful promise: "We know that in all things God works for the good of those who love him, who have been called according to his purpose" (Rom 8:28 NIV).

Some who hold to the blueprint worldview have concluded from this verse that God *causes* everything for our good. While this interpretation is grammatically possible, it's not required. And this, I believe, is fortunate. The blueprint interpretation would require us to affirm that the death of Melanie's baby was for her own good, the death of the couple's son was for their own good, and the death of each Christian in the World Trade Center and Pentagon attacks was for their own good. *This* is reassuring? Such an interpretation would contradict the biblical teaching. that human and angelic beings have their own free will and cause many things to happen that are against God's will. Indeed, it stands in tension with the central thrust of Jesus' warfare ministry.

The promise Paul gives is that "*in* all things"—whatever or whoever caused them—"God *works for* the good." Wherever we find ourselves and however we got there, we can know that God is already at work to bring good out of it. Those who place their trust in God are called to work with him to bring redemptive meaning out of every event, however tragic it may be. Though our suffering may be the result of a multitude of free decisions—a drunk driver on our street just when our child is chasing her ball, for example—the suffering need not be meaningless. In his infinite wisdom God has been anticipating and preparing for this very possibility from the foundation of the world. Thus with a tender creativity we can scarcely begin to imagine, he is able to bring redemptive value out of the most tragic and meaningless events. In the midst of all things God is working with us for our good. But we need not assume that he is the *cause* or the *ultimate reason* behind all things.

Many people can't imagine how God could bring good out of evil when he wasn't involved in bringing the event to pass in the first place. Perhaps they can see how God has used the tragedy to benefit their life and thus conclude that God orchestrated it for this purpose. While this is understandable, given God's amazing redemptive wisdom, these people don't realize that they are actually *limiting* God in drawing this conclusion. They are overlooking God's ability to perfectly anticipate and prepare for *possibilities* with the same confidence he anticipates *certain-*

ties. Finite humans would need to orchestrate everything to bring the good out of bad events, so they assume *God* must need to orchestrate everything. But he doesn't. And it's this mistaken assumption that leads people to conclude that not only is God working *in* all things for the good but he is also *behind* all events of history.

This mistake creates an experience-based picture of God rather than a Christ-centered one. It compromises the clarity of our knowledge of God in Christ with the ambiguity of the war-torn creation. The result: many live less passionately than they otherwise would, and others abandon faith in God altogether. This is entirely unnecessary. If we simply trust God's infinite wisdom, keep our eyes focused on Christ and yield to God's loving presence, we can be confident that our suffering is not meaningless.

PRINCIPLE 4: LET GO OF THE "WHY" QUESTION AND CONFRONT EVIL

Conditioned by the blueprint worldview, Western Christians obsessively ask why suffering happens to them. This is in most circumstances an utterly useless and unanswerable question. The variables that contributed to any particular episode of suffering extend throughout history and may have nothing whatsoever to do with the wills of the people afflicted or with God's will for their life.

Moreover, the "why" question was systematically discouraged by Jesus, by the psalmist and by the author of Job. Jesus said we don't need to wonder why a tower fell on some people but not others, why certain people were massacred but not others, or why a man was born blind. We only need to repent of our sin and seek to glorify God (Lk 13:1-5; Jn 9:1-5). Moreover, not once in his ministry to the afflicted did Jesus ever inquire how or why their condition came about.

When you find yourself or a loved one in the midst of suffering, it's almost always wise to let go of the "why" question. To be sure, there are situations where we need to assign responsibility for a wrong done in order to rectify it. But even in these situations, once the situation is rectified, it's wise to let go of any further "why" questions.

For example, if there were obvious things you willfully did to bring suffering on yourself or another, *you* are the ultimate reason behind the suffering. Though it's true that there is an unfathomably complex set of factors that contributed to what you did, you bear primary responsibility to the extent that you acted of your own free will. Thus you need to acknowledge your responsibility, take whatever action is necessary to remedy the wrong and learn from it. But having done this, it's necessary to let any further "why" questions go. Instead, you need to fix your eyes on Jesus, trust in God's forgiveness and get on with the business of living.

Similarly, if there is another person who is responsible for your suffering, this needs to be acknowledged and action needs to be taken to rectify the situation as much as possible. But having done all you can do, it's important to forgive this person and release the matter to God. Remember you're also a sinner, and God, not you, is the judge of people. There is no appropriate or helpful place for vengeance. When we hang on to grievances and "why" questions too long, they begin to control us. Paul says that anger harbored in our heart makes "room for the devil" (Eph 4:26-27). Like a cancer, bitterness grows and consumes our capacity for passionate living, joy and peace. Whether it's asked for or not, extend God's forgiveness to the person, let the matter go and get on with life.

Aside from certain circumstances (as in the two examples above), it's impossible to answer "why" questions. "If only we hadn't let our son take his seat belt off." "If we had prayed more." "If we hadn't slept in." "If a demon hadn't been available or a butterfly hadn't flapped its wings." Such questions are as useless as they are unanswerable. Even if you could find an answer—which is to say, even if you were omniscient—it wouldn't alleviate your suffering. The question we ought to ask is not, Why did this happen like this? but rather, What can God, others and I do *now* to alleviate the pain of this situation and bring redemptive value out of it?

One of the most unfortunate consequences of the blueprint worldview is that people are inclined to accept things as coming from God that aren't from God at all. As Jesus modeled and taught us, we ought to aggressively storm the gates of Hades (Mt 16:18). When we confront circumstances that reflect the will of Satan, we are to do everything possible to bring them into conformity with God's will. We aren't called to accept everything *as* God's will; instead, we are called to transform everything to bring it into conformity *with* God's will. Only when we live with this mindset can we claim to be *doing* God's will.

PRINCIPLE 5: LIVING IN THE SPIRIT

In a world of ambiguity, how can we determine what God's will is? More specifically, how are we to know what we should accept as good and what we should confront as evil? How do we know when God is at work, when Satan is at work or when a set of circumstances are the chance result of a myriad factors?

Note that these are questions we have to live with *whatever worldview we embrace.* They don't present themselves only to people who adopt a warfare worldview. Even those who believe that everything unfolds according to a divine blueprint have a daily struggle with discerning God's will. They still have to discern what should be accepted or confronted in their life. Believing that everything ultimately happens for a divine reason doesn't eliminate these questions. Therefore the blueprint perspective has no advantage. By contrast, I believe that acknowledging the incomprehensible complexity of the world helps us as we struggle with these questions.

The most fundamental guidance the New Testament offers us is that we must "live by the Spirit" (Gal 5:16).[1] All Christians have God's Spirit dwelling within them, and he wants to direct our lives on a daily basis (Rom 8:9). All who are "led by the Spirit of God are children of God" (Rom 8:14). We are to "live in the Spirit" and be "guided by the Spirit" (Gal 5:25). While we know God's general will for us in Jesus Christ and through Scripture, usually we don't know God's *specific* will for *particular* circumstances except through the Spirit. The Spirit alone knows the mind of God, and he will lead us if we are willing to listen (1 Cor 2:10-11).

We are members of the body of Christ, who is our head (1 Cor 12:27; Eph 1:22-23; 4:11-15, 5:23; Col 1:18; 2:18-19). A body's members operate by listening to and being obedient to their head. So it is with believers in relation to Christ, our head. Jesus Christ leads and guides us through his Spirit. Only as we walk with the Spirit do we carry out the desires of the head. Using a biblical analogy, we are like soldiers stationed in a foreign country who must not get so "entangled in everyday affairs" that we stop being attentive to the moment by moment commands of our "enlisting officer," Jesus Christ (2 Tim 2:4).

We see this principle illustrated in the early church. For example, Philip struck up a conversation with a particular man because the Spirit told him to "go over to this chariot and join it" (Acts 8:29). Peter undoubtedly would have refused the invitation of three Gentiles had not the Spirit told him to do otherwise (Acts 10:19; 11:12). Paul and Timothy would have taken their evangelistic ministry to Asia Minor were it not for the fact that they were "forbidden by the Holy Spirit" (Acts 16:6). Similarly, they would have taken their missionary endeavors to Bithynia except for the fact that "the Spirit of Jesus did not allow them" (Acts 16:7). And following the model of Jesus, Paul would have continued to pray against the thorn in his flesh had not the Lord told him to stop (2 Cor 12:8-10). The point is that the New Testament never assumes people can figure out on their own what God's specific will may be in every particular situation.

Some people assume that if God's will doesn't determine everything, he must be distant. Operating out of an all-or-nothing mindset, they conclude that history must unfold capriciously, without God's involvement. But the exact opposite is the case. When we understand that our complex world doesn't unfold according to a meticulous blueprint, we can appreciate how necessary it is for God to be involved at every turn. Were it not for God's continual involvement, the world would be utterly chaotic, and we couldn't be assured of ultimate victory over evil. The blueprint view, not the warfare view, tends to distance God from the events of life.

In the same way, understanding that life is unfathomably complex encourages us—indeed, forces us—to listen to God on a moment by moment basis. When we appreciate all the variables that lie behind every situation, we become fully aware that there is no way we could figure out the right thing to do on our own.[2] Living in this sea of ambiguity, we realize that we need to look for God's guidance all the time. There is no fixed set of principles, no exhaustive rule book, that covers all of life's situations. And this is to our advantage, for it forces us to constantly attend to our relationship with God—which is, after all, the central point of our life.

PRINCIPLE 6: LIVE IN HOPE KNOWING IT ALL WILL BE WORTH IT

One of the reasons why we like simplistic answers to difficult questions is that we don't like ambiguity. As Job insightfully saw, much of the abusive theology his friends were hurling at him was motivated by their own fear (Job 6:21). They hated the way Job's suffering called into question their God-in-a-box theology, and they feared that what happened to Job might happen to them. Hence, despite all appearances they insisted that the universe was a fair place, that fortune and misfortune are God's just rewards and punishments, and that Job's suffering must be his own fault.

A central point of the book of Job is to denounce this theology. But this means that the universe is not a fair place. It means that we ultimately can't know why a righteous person like Job suffers. And it therefore means coming to terms with our fear of living in a sea of ambiguity.

The Bible never assures us things will go well for us in this life. To the contrary, the New Testament teaches us that Christ's followers should *expect* to suffer (Jn 16:33; 1 Thess 3:4). If Christ suffered, those who model their life after him must expect the same (2 Pet 1:21). Paul assumes that hardship, distress, persecution, famine, nakedness, peril and execution can happen to a believer (Rom 8:35). He assumes that angels, rulers and powers are at work against us and can negatively influence our lives

(Rom 8:39; see also Eph 6:12). He goes so far as to apply Psalm 44:22 to the life of believers: "For your sake we are being killed all day long; we are accounted as sheep to be slaughtered" (Rom 8:36).

This is hardly encouraging for those who view life from a strictly human point of view. So long as a person's internal tranquillity is conditioned by life's circumstances, they can't help but be fearful. This is precisely why the New Testament doesn't attempt to assuage our fears by falsely reassuring us that our life will always be fine, or that it is orchestrated by God. To the contrary, the New Testament concedes that the entire creation is groaning in pain because it is under a curse (Rom 8:19-22).

What the New Testament offers us is a peace in the midst of the sea of ambiguity we swim in. Scripture offers us the peace of knowing that Christ is with us in all circumstances. The Holy Spirit gives us supernatural fearlessness in the midst of all circumstances. And it offers us the assurance that God is at work to bring good out of all circumstances. But we have yet to discuss the most decisive assurance the New Testament gives us: heaven.

Jesus Christ died, and in this painful sea of ambiguity we participate in his sufferings and death (Rom 6:3-5; 8:16-18; 1 Cor 4:9-12; Col 1:24). But Jesus also rose from the dead. And just as his atoning death provides the key to understanding who we are before God, his resurrection provides the key to understanding what we will be before God. Though we are afflicted now, we know that because he conquered sin, death and the devil, we too will ultimately overcome them. We too will be raised from the dead and will eternally live and reign in his unsurpassable love and joy.

This promise transforms everything. It alters how we view ourselves and transforms how we see the world. This is why, in the midst of recounting the trials of his life, Paul proclaimed, "in all these things we are more than conquerors through him who loved us" (Rom 8:37). Not just conquerors—as though we temporarily overcome these trials—but *more than conquerors*. If we keep our eyes focused on Jesus, "we can never be separated from the love of God in Christ Jesus our Lord" (Rom 8:39).

When we or someone we encounter is suffering, it's crucial that we assess it from an eternal perspective. The war that plagues this creation will someday cease: we need to dream about heaven. God's glorious plan for creation will one day be fulfilled. Christ will unambiguously reign as Lord over the earth through us, his mediators. God's triune love and sovereign providence will be extended and displayed through us as we align our wills with his in love. We will co-rule with him (2 Tim 2:12; Rev 5:10; 20:6; 22:5) and eternally share in his love, joy and glory throughout eternity (Jn 17:20-25).

God will rule on the earth—a new earth. Heaven is not a place in the clouds but a perfected version of the world we live in now. John gives us an inspired portrayal of heaven:

> Then I saw a new heaven and a new earth; for the first heaven and the first earth had passed away, and the sea was no more. And I saw the holy city, the new Jerusalem, coming down out of heaven from God, prepared as a bride adorned for her husband. And I heard a loud voice from the throne saying,
>
> > "See, the home of God is among mortals.
> > He will dwell with them as their God;
> > they will be his peoples,
> > and God himself will be with them;
> > he will wipe every tear from their eyes.
> > Death will be no more;
> > mourning and crying and pain will be no more,
> > for the first things have passed away."
>
> And the one who was seated on the throne said, "See, I am making all things new. . . . To the thirsty I will give water as a gift from the spring of the water of life. Those who conquer will inherit these things, and I will be their God and they will be my children." (Rev 21:1-7)

God's "home" will be our home. God will be with us as loving Father, and we will be his children. The earth will be rid of everything that is inconsistent with his loving will: sin, sorrow, sickness and death. All things will be reconciled to God through Christ (Col 1:20; see also Acts 3:21). All things will be made new. All things will be "gathered up in [Christ]" (Eph 1:10). And, as it has always been planned, the triune God will be "all in all" (1 Cor 15:28). When all opposition to God is removed, we will continually live in the presence of his triune love. All our desires that are frustrated in this war-torn epoch will be fulfilled. Being partakers of God's triune love, we will be in want of nothing.

However difficult life in the war zone is—and for some, it is unthinkably difficult—it will be worth it for those who trust in Christ. Indeed, the Bible says it will be *more* than worth it. The "sufferings of this present time are not worth comparing with the glory about to be revealed to us" (Rom 8:18). There is no comparison between the suffering of this world and the eternal glory that awaits those who are Christ's. In light of the unthinkable horror some people undergo, heaven has got to be one unfathomably wonderful place!

The most fundamental and profound hope the Bible gives us is not that everything *now* follows God's will but that *someday* God's purposes will be done on earth as they are in heaven. While we certainly shouldn't be so heavenly minded that we're no earthly good, we nevertheless need to take time to ponder and enjoy the glory that awaits all who trust in Christ. Someday, Christ himself will wipe away every tear from our eyes. Reminding ourselves of this promise helps us cope with the tears of the ambiguous, war-torn present.

If we savor it deeply, a vision of heaven eradicates all fear of pain and death. While it answers none of the "why" questions that arise in this capricious war zone, it does something much more profound. Heaven renders unanswerable "why" questions irrelevant and inspires us to live with them in hope.

EIGHT

MERCY AND HARDENING

All significant theories confront data that can be interpreted as counting against them. No theory, whether in science or theology, explains all the data with equal aplomb. This is true in theology in general and with the warfare worldview in particular. There are some biblical data that, at least in the view of some, conflict with it.

Every theory must attempt to explain apparently discordant data as best as it can. This is what I will attempt to do in the last two chapters of this book. I will examine the key biblical passages that some people believe support the blueprint perspective and that thereby suggest that the warfare worldview is misguided.

THE BLUEPRINT INTERPRETATION OF ROMANS 9

Some people believe Romans 9 demonstrates that God saves and damns whichever individuals he wants to.[1] Clearly if this is the case, any view that emphasizes the free will of created beings (e.g., the warfare worldview) is in trouble.

On first glance, it may seem that the blueprint interpretation has a strong case. For in Romans 9 Paul explicitly says that God "has mercy on whomever he chooses, and he hardens the heart of whomever he chooses" (Rom 9:18). Paul illustrates God's sovereign election by referring to God's choice of Isaac over Ishmael (Rom 9:7-8) and of Jacob over

Esau (Rom 9:10-13). Regarding this latter choice Paul writes:

> Even before [Jacob and Esau] had been born or had done anything
> good or bad (so that God's purpose of election might continue, not
> by works but by his call) [Rebecca] was told, "The elder shall serve
> the younger." As it is written,
>> "I have loved Jacob,
>>   but I have hated Esau." (Rom 9:11-13)

Without regard to anything Jacob or Esau did, God chose to "love" Jacob
and "hate" Esau. Thus Paul concludes that God's choice of people "depends
not on human will or exertion, but on God who shows mercy" (Rom 9:16).

Support for the blueprint interpretation seems to grow even stronger
as Paul goes on to depict God's relationship to humans as a potter to his
clay. God has the right to fashion us, his clay, however he sees fit. And
this is precisely what he does:

> Has the potter no right over the clay, to make out of the same lump
> one object for special use and another for ordinary use? What if
> God, desiring to show his wrath and to make known his power,
> has endured with much patience the objects of wrath that are
> made for destruction; and what if he has done so in order to make
> known the riches of his glory for the objects of mercy, which he has
> prepared beforehand for glory? (Rom 9:21-23)

According to some blueprint theorists, Paul is teaching that God simply fashions some vessels for destruction in order to display his wrath
and power, and other vessels for mercy in order to display his glory. He
hardens the former and has mercy on the latter. And this hardening and
granting mercy is not based on anything God finds in the vessel. It is
simply based on God's free decision. If this seems unfair, as it undoubtedly does, Paul responds by invalidating the sentiment: "Who indeed are
you, a human being, to argue with God? Will what is molded say to the
one who molds it, 'Why have you made me like this?' " (Rom 9:20).

I call this interpretation of Romans 9 the "blueprint interpretation" because it holds that some become hardened and others receive mercy according to God's eternal blueprint. From this perspective unbelief and belief are part of God's plan. It's evident that if this interpretation is correct, the warfare worldview I've been defending must be mistaken. But I don't believe that the blueprint interpretation is correct. In what follows I offer six considerations that I believe demonstrate the incorrectness of this understanding of Romans 9.[2]

THE ABSOLUTENESS OF CHRIST AND THE UNIVERSALITY OF GOD'S LOVE

First, the view that God unilaterally determines some humans to be forever outside his saving grace contradicts the revelation of God in Jesus Christ. Indeed, it renders God's self-revelation on Calvary penultimate. The unconditional love and judgment on sin manifested on the cross are qualified by a "more foundational revelation" of God's eternal selection.

On this supposition, the revelation of God in Christ only tells half the story; the other half tells of a dark streak in God whereby he arbitrarily fashions some people to be "objects of wrath made for destruction" and others to be "objects of mercy . . . prepared beforehand for glory" (Rom 9:22-23). He then eternally punishes the objects of wrath (for being the way he designed them to be) in contrast to his gracious treatment of the vessels of mercy.

If this is so, we must conclude that

1. Christ is not the one, absolute, definitive, sufficient revelation of God.

2. He is not the one and only Word, image and exact imprint of God (Jn 1:1; Col 1:15; Heb 1:3).

3. He doesn't sum up everything about God for us and everything about us for God.

4. There is a more fundamental and sinister "word" of God concealed by the word God speaks in Christ.

We must also conclude that behind the image of God dying in love for humanity is the real God who creates many humans for the sole purpose of displaying his eternal wrath. The beautiful good news of God's outrageous love in Christ conceals the horrifying bad news of God's equally outrageous hatred. If this is so, we must conclude that God so loved *some of* the world (contra Jn 3:16) that he gave his only Son. The rest are being prepared for eternal wrath and destruction.

On the other hand, if we view Jesus as our definitive picture of God, qualified by none other, then we must conclude there is something amiss with the blueprint interpretation of Romans 9. For Christ reveals and the biblical witness confirms that God is love: his love is universal, impartial and kind, and he desires all to be saved (e.g., Deut 10:17-19; 2 Chron 19:7; Ezek 18:25; Mk 12:14; Jn 3:16; Acts 10:34; Rom 2:10-11; Eph 6:9; 1 Tim 2:4; 1 Pet 1:17; 2 Pet 3:9; 1 Jn 4:8).

HAS GOD BROKEN COVENANT?

Second, the blueprint interpretation assumes that Paul is concerned with individual salvation in Romans 9. But this is not the issue Paul is addressing. The expressed issue is whether or not "the word of God had failed" (Rom 9:6). That is, has God's covenant with the Jews been rescinded?

To many Jews this shocking conclusion seemed to follow from the gospel Paul was preaching. Most Jews of the day understood God's covenantal faithfulness to depend on two things: their nationality and their external obedience to the law. If what Paul was preaching was true—that is, if salvation was available to anyone, including Gentiles, simply on the basis of faith—then neither Jewish nationality nor obedience to the law counted for anything (see Gal 5:6). It seemed that the uniqueness of the Jewish identity and calling had been undermined.

Even worse, Paul's gospel now seemed to be working against them. Because the Jews strove for righteousness based on the external observation of the law (works) instead of faith, they were now being hardened (Rom 9:18)—evidenced by the fact that so few believed in Jesus (Rom

9:31-32). This meant that the very people to whom God made covenant promises were now being hardened. Hence it looked as if "the word of God had failed."

This is the question Paul is addressing in Romans 9 (as well as chapters 10—11). It's a question of God's fidelity to Israel as a covenant partner. It has nothing to do with how God elects individuals to salvation.

ELECTION TO SERVICE, NOT SALVATION

The way Paul answers this objection also shows that his concern is with God's relationship with a nation, not with individual salvation. Paul refutes the idea that God's covenantal promises failed by showing that they were never based on nationality or external obedience to the law. Rather, Paul argues, God always exercised his sovereign right to choose whomever he wanted to choose.

Paul illustrates this point by referring to God's choice of Isaac over Ishmael and Jacob over Esau without consideration of their attributes or merits (Rom 9:8-13). These decisions were made ahead of time, were not wholly unexpected, reversed primogeniture and involved individuals who were not exemplary in their character. To top it off, Isaac was conceived supernaturally.

In offering these examples Paul is defending God's right to choose whomever he wants by any means he chooses. Thus, it shouldn't be shocking to Jews to discover that God is choosing to establish a covenant that includes anyone—even Gentiles—based simply on their faith. But in using Isaac and Jacob to illustrate God's prerogative to choose, Paul is not concerned with the eternal destiny of people but rather with God's sovereignty in electing people *to a historical vocation.*

To underscore God's sovereign prerogative, Paul emphasizes the arbitrary way God brought about a chosen people, through Isaac and Jacob, whose mission was to serve God and the world as a nation of priests (Ex 19:6; Is 61:6) and a "light to all the nations" (Is 42:6; 49:6; 60:3). Israel was to be the means by which all the nations of the world would be blessed.[3] Their election as a nation was always primarily about service—not individual salvation.

Paul emphasizes the arbitrariness of God's choice of the Jews to unsettle those who would think God's word had failed because their nationality and external observation to the law had been rendered irrelevant in Christ. Throughout Romans 9—11 Paul is at pains to show that God's goal all along was to reach beyond the borders of Israel and win the whole world (Rom 9:25-26, 33; 10:10-21; 11:11-12). Indeed, Paul insists that God would yet attain his goal, but since Israel as a nation rejected the Messiah, God would use their blindness rather than their obedience to reach the nations (Rom 11:11-32).

We are clearly reading too much into Romans 9 if we think that Paul is suggesting that Ishmael or Esau—or anyone else not chosen as God formed the Jewish nation—were individually damned. Paul is simply not concerned here with individual destinies. Indeed, his examples are chosen precisely because they represent more than individuals—they represent nations. In choosing Isaac over Ishmael and Jacob over Esau, God illustrated his choice of Israel (descendants of Isaac and Jacob) over the Moabites (descendants of Ishmael) and the Edomites (descendants of Esau). Again, this doesn't mean that all Moabites and Edomites were eternally lost; it simply means that these nations would not serve the priestly role in history that God chose the Israelites for.

This national focus is emphasized by Paul's citation of Malachi 1:2-3, "I have loved Jacob, but I have hated Esau" (Rom 9:13), which is explicitly about the country of Edom. Some might suppose that God's pronouncement of "love" for Jacob and "hatred" for Esau shows that he is speaking about their individual eternal destinies, but this is mistaken. In Hebraic thought, when "love" and "hate" are contrasted they usually are meant hyperbolically. The expression simply means to strongly prefer one person or thing over another.

So, for example, when Jesus said, "Whoever comes to me and does not hate father and mother, wife and children, brothers and sisters, yes, and even life itself, cannot be my disciple" (Lk 14:26), he was not saying we should literally hate our family. Elsewhere he taught people to love and respect their parents (Mk 10:19), which the Old Testament also taught. Indeed, he commanded us to love our enemies (Mt 5:44)! Jesus was saying that *he* must be preferred above parents, spouses, children, siblings and even life itself. The meaning of Malachi's phrase, then, is simply that God preferred Israel over Edom as his covenant people.

Hence, there is no justification for interpreting Romans 9 as though it were trying to teach us about how God saves or damns individuals.

PAUL'S SUMMARY AND FREE WILL

A fourth argument that demonstrates the error of the blueprint interpretation concerns Paul's summary at the end of Romans 9. Whenever we are struggling to understand a complex line of reasoning, it's crucial to pay close attention to the author's own summary, assuming one is provided. By all accounts Romans 9 is a difficult, complex and highly disputed passage. Fortunately, Paul provides us with a very clear summary of his argument. Unfortunately for the blueprint interpretation, it appeals to free will as the decisive factor in determining who "receives mercy" and who gets "hardened."

Paul begins his summary by asking, "What then shall we say?" (v. 30). If the blueprint interpretation were correct, we would expect Paul to answer by saying something like, "The sovereign God has determined who will be elect and who will not, and no one has the right to question him." However, Paul doesn't say anything like this. Instead, he summarizes his argument by saying:

> Gentiles, who did not strive for righteousness, have attained it, that is, righteousness through faith; but Israel, who did strive for the righteousness that is based on the law, did not succeed in fulfilling that law. Why not? *Because they did not strive for it on the basis of faith, but as if it were based on works.* (Rom 9:30-32, italics added)

This is extremely significant. Paul explains everything he's been talking about in Romans 9 by appealing to the morally responsible choices of the Israelites and Gentiles. The one thing God has always looked for in people is faith. The Jews did not "strive" by faith, though they should have (Rom 10:3). They chose to trust in their own works. The Gentiles, however, simply believed that God would justify them by faith. This theme recurs throughout chapters 9—11. As a nation, Paul says, the Jews "were broken off because of their unbelief" (Rom 11:20). This is why they have been hardened (Rom 11:7, 25) while the Gentiles who sought God by faith have been "grafted in" (Rom 11:23).

We see that God's process of hardening some and having mercy on others is not arbitrary: God expresses "severity toward those who have fallen [the nation of Israel] but kindness toward you [believers], provided you continue in his kindness" (Rom 11:22). God has mercy on people and hardens people *in response to their belief or unbelief.* And he is willing to change his mind about both the hardening and the mercy when people change. If Gentiles become arrogant and cease walking by faith alone, they will once again be "cut off." And if the Jews who are now hardened will not "persist in their unbelief," God will "graft them in again" (Rom 11:22-23).

To the Jews who trusted in their national identity and external obedience to the law, this hardening *seemed* arbitrary. But Paul chides them by asking, "Who indeed are you, a human being, to argue with God? Will what is molded say to the one who molds it, 'Why have you made me like this?'" (Rom 9:20). But as Paul makes abundantly clear throughout Romans 9—11, the hardening was not arbitrary. It was perfectly consistent with the criteria of faith God has always used. He gives mercy in response to faith and he hardens in response to unbelief. Only people who were convinced that national identity and good works were the basis of God's mercy would think that God was now being arbitrary.

THE FLEXIBLE POTTER AND WILLING CLAY
Fifth, if read in the light of its Old Testament background, Paul's analogy

of a potter working with clay doesn't imply that the potter unilaterally decides everything, as the blueprint interpretation of Romans 9 suggests. Indeed, in the Old Testament passage that makes the most use of the potter-clay analogy, it has the exact opposite meaning.

In Jeremiah 18 the Lord shows Jeremiah a potter who is molding a vessel that doesn't turn out right. So the potter revises his plan and forms a different kind of pot out of it (Jer 18:1-4). In the same way, since the Lord is the potter and Israel is the clay, he has the right and is willing to "change his mind" about his plans for Israel if they repent (Jer 18:4-11). Indeed, the Lord announced that whenever he's about to judge a nation, he is willing to change his mind if the nation repents. Conversely, whenever God is about to bless a nation, he'll change his mind if that nation turns away from him. In other words, the point of the potter-clay analogy is not God's unilateral control, but God's willingness and right to change his plans in response to changed hearts.

The passage fits perfectly with the point Paul makes in Romans 9. While some individual Jews had accepted Jesus as the Messiah, the nation as a whole had rejected Jesus and God's purpose (cf. Lk 7:30). Though God had previously blessed Israel, he had changed his mind about them and was hardening them. Ironically and shockingly, the Jews were finding themselves in the same position as their old nemesis Pharaoh. He had hardened his heart toward God, so God responded by hardening Pharaoh further in order to enhance God's own sovereign purposes (Rom 9:17). So too, Paul is arguing, God was now hardening the Jews in their self-chosen unbelief to further his sovereign purposes. He was going to use their rebellion to do what he had always hoped their obedience would do, namely, bring the non-Jewish world to him (Rom 11:11-12).

Even here, however, the sovereign potter remains flexible. If the Jews abandon their unbelief—clearly God's hardening is not determinative or irrevocable—the potter will once again refashion his plan. Conversely, if the Gentiles abandon their belief and become prideful—clearly God's mercy is not determinative or irrevocable—the potter will once again re-fashion his plan for them and cut them off (Rom 11:12-25).

We see that the point of the potter analogy is the opposite of what the blueprint theorists would have us believe. The sovereign potter has the right to revise his plans in response to the clay, which is exactly what God was doing to the nation of Israel. However arbitrary God's revisions appear to Jews, those revisions are in fact perfectly wise and just.

This sheds light on why Paul responds to the charge that God is unfair by quoting God: "I will have mercy on whom I have mercy" (Rom 9:15; see also v. 18). He isn't suggesting that God shows mercy to or hardens people without any consideration of the choices they make. To the con-trary, the people God chooses to have mercy on are those who have faith, whether they are Jews or Gentiles. And the people he hardens are those who don't "strive for [righteousness] on the basis of faith, but as if it were based on works" (Rom 9:32). But to Jews who insisted that God chooses people based on their nationality or works, God's right to have mercy on whomever he wishes needed to be emphasized.

The original context of the Old Testament quotation Paul uses is also significant. While Moses was receiving the Ten Commandments on Mt. Sinai, the Jews turned away from God to worship idols (Ex 32:1-6). God responded by telling Moses he was going to destroy Israel and completely start over with Moses (Ex 32:9-10). Because of Moses' intercession, however, the Lord changed his mind and gave the Israel-ites a chance to repent (Ex 32:14-35). The flexible potter refashioned his plan.

Following this episode the Lord revealed some of his glory to Moses, saying, "I will have mercy on whom I will have mercy" (Ex 33:19 NIV). The Lord shows mercy to people of faith like Moses, but he judges re-bellious people like Israel and Pharaoh. By choosing to have faith in God or to rebel against God, individuals decide their fate. They determine whether God will fashion them into vessels of mercy or vessels prepared for destruction (Rom 9:21-23).

This also explains why Paul says that God "endured with much patience" the vessels he was preparing for destruction (Rom 9:22). Why would God have to be patient with rebellious people if he was the one making them rebellious in the first place? Why would he go on to say, "All day long I have held out my hands to a disobedient and contrary people" (Rom 10:21, quoting Is 65:2) if he was the one molding them to be disobedient? And why would a God of love intentionally fashion people to rebel against him and bring destruction on themselves in the first place?

In point of fact, the potter is patient with the vessels being prepared for destruction because it's not his original will to destroy them. He would love all "disobedient and contrary people" to come to him, and thus he's patient with them. He doesn't want anyone to perish but longs for all to be saved (2 Pet 3:9). But so long as they persist in their unbelief, they remain vessels fit for destruction.

IT'S ABOUT WISDOM, NOT POWER

This leads to our sixth and final point. When Paul responds to the charge of injustice by asking, "who . . . are you, a human being, to argue with God?" (Rom 9:20), he's not thereby appealing to the sheer power of the potter over the clay. He is rather appealing to the sovereign wisdom of the potter in refashioning clay in a manner that fits the kind of clay he has to work with. When a person yields to his influence and has faith, God fashions a vessel of honor. When we become "spoiled" (Jer 18:4) and resist God's will, he fashions a vessel for destruction.

This fashioning *looks* arbitrary to Jews who believed that they were vessels of honor. But they didn't "strive for [God's righteousness] on the basis of faith, but as if it were based on works" (Rom 9:32). To these people Paul sarcastically asks, "Who are you?" In truth, God's fashioning is not arbitrary at all. It's based on whether or not they are willing to seek after the righteousness of God that comes by faith, not works (Rom 9:30-32; 10:3-5, 12-13; 11:22-23).

CONCLUSION

On the basis of these six considerations I conclude that the blueprint interpretation of Romans 9 is misguided and unfortunate. It is misguided not only because it misinterprets Paul but because it fundamentally clashes with the supremacy of God's self-revelation in Christ. And it is unfortunate because it tragically replaces the glorious picture of God in Christ loving undeserving sinners with a picture of a deity who arbitrarily fashions people for eternal destruction—and then punishes them for being that way. It exchanges the picture of a beautiful God who reigns supreme in self-sacrificial love and flexible wisdom for a picture of an arbitrary God who reigns by sheer power.

With Paul, those who embrace the biblical warfare worldview can unequivocally affirm that the sovereign God "has mercy on whomever he wants to have mercy, and he hardens whomever he wants to harden." Along with Paul we believe that the "whomever" he has mercy on refers to "all who choose to believe" while the "whomever" he hardens refers to "all who refuse to believe." The passage demonstrates the wisdom of God's loving flexibility, not the sheer determinism of God's power.

PROVIDENCE AND CONTROL

In the last chapter I responded to the foundational biblical support (Rom 9) for the strong form of the blueprint worldview. In this final chapter I examine nine other key passages or sets of passages that supposedly support the blueprint worldview and thus contradict the warfare worldview.[1]

THE LORD DOES WHATEVER HE PLEASES

Whatever the Lord pleases he does,

in heaven and on earth. (Ps 135:6)

Some conclude from this passage and others like it (Job 23:13-14; 42:2; Ps 115:3; Dan 4:35) that God's will can never be thwarted. Whatever God wants, God gets. As Augustine put it, "the will of the omnipotent is always undefeated." But since (1) Jesus' life, death and resurrection reveal God's unequivocal stance against sin and his willingness to suffer at the hands of sinners, (2) Scripture explicitly teaches that God's will is sometimes thwarted (Is 63:10; Lk 7:30; Acts 7:51; Eph 4:30; Heb 3:8, 15; 4:7), and (3) the denial that God's will can be thwarted leads to the conclusion that God actually wills every aspect of the horrendous evil we find in the world, I submit we should seek an alternative interpretation of these verses.

These passages certainly teach that the Lord can do whatever he pleases, but they don't assert that the Lord is pleased to control everything. Why should we assume that God desires to do everything he has the raw power to do? Parents have the power to completely control their young children. But emotionally healthy parents refrain from doing so. Though it involves an element of risk, good parents allow their children a certain degree of freedom so they can grow up to be healthy, responsible, decision-making adults. So too Scripture makes it evident that though God *could* control us, he desires to empower us to be self-determining, morally responsible agents. "Whatever the Lord pleases he does," *including* creating free agents.

Those who believe that God meticulously controls everything often claim that their view of God is the only one that depicts God as truly sovereign and glorious. There are different ways of being sovereign, however, and some are more virtuous than others. For example, who do you most admire? Those who lead by controlling as much as they can, or those who lead by empowering and influencing others by virtue of their character and wisdom? Obviously, the latter is more virtuous and praiseworthy. Why then should we think that God would be more glorious if he exercised meticulous control?

Again, I concede that God could control everything if he wanted to. He's omnipotent, and creation is, after all, his. But what would be praiseworthy about this display of raw power? I can wiggle my fingers at will because they are *my* fingers. But few would praise me for displaying this "power." So too, God could wiggle his creation any way he chose, for it's *his creation.* But would this display of power be more glorious than God empowering other agents to have say-so and seeking to influence them by his love?

I submit that when we think about God's sovereignty and glory in the light of Calvary, we won't be inclined to define God's sovereignty in terms of meticulous control. God can indeed do whatever he wants to do, as biblical authors uniformly proclaim. But as unexpected as it may be to our fallen "natural minds," Christ reveals that the omnipotent God fundamentally wants to enter into a freely chosen love relationship with people. And he's willing to allow these very people to crucify him to win them over with his love.

THE LORD CREATES WEAL AND WOE

"I form light and create darkness,

  I make weal and create woe;

  I the Lord do all these things." (Is 45:7)

Who can command and have it done

  if the Lord has not ordained it?

Is it not from the mouth of the Most High

  that good and bad come? (Lam 3:37-38)

Some defenders of the blueprint worldview argue that these passages (see also Amos 3:6) attribute both good and evil, light and darkness, to God's sovereign hand. Hence, they encourage us to see tragedies like the 9/11 attacks as fitting into God's sovereign purposes. Four things may be said in response to this, however.

First, if we accept the blueprint interpretation of these verses, how can we escape the logical conclusion that God is partly evil? If these passages teach that God brings about good and evil, it seems we should accept that God is partly good and partly evil. Why obfuscate the issue by maintaining that God is all good despite the fact that he brings forth evil? Blueprint theologians want to avoid this conclusion, of course, because the belief that God is all holy and all good is foundational to the Christian faith. If it is impossible to conceive of a good tree bringing forth bad fruit or a good heart bringing forth evil deeds, as Jesus taught, it is just as impossible to conceive of an all-good God bringing forth evil (Mt 7:16-18). For all their erudite distinctions between primary and secondary causes, necessary and contingent effects, and so on, no blueprint theologian has ever adequately explained how God can infallibly bring about evil while remaining all good, and while holding other agents morally responsible for the evil he ultimately brings about.[2]

Second, the suggestion that God is secretly behind evil contradicts the revelation of God in Christ. In Jesus' life, death and resurrection we see God confronting and overcoming the devil, light confronting and overcoming darkness, love confronting and overcoming hate, holiness confronting and overcoming sin, and life confronting and overcoming death. This revelation must not be placed alongside of and qualified in the light of a deterministic interpretation of several verses from the Old Testament. Rather, as the one Word, image, exact imprint and visible manifestation of God, all previous or extracanonical revelations must be *read in the light of Christ* (Jn 1:1, 18; 14:7-10; Col 1:15; Heb 1:3; see also Jn 5:39-47). Thus whatever else we make of these Old Testament passages, they can't modify the unequivocal opposition between good and evil revealed in Christ.

Third, the revelation of God in Christ is consistent with and fulfills the anticipatory revelation of God throughout Scripture. Not surprisingly, then, the view that God is secretly behind evil contradicts a major motif of Scripture. The Bible teaches that God is perfect love (1 Jn 4:18) and "does not willingly afflict, or grieve anyone" (Lam 3:33). It tells us that "all [God's] ways are just" and there is no deceit in him (Deut 32:4). It reveals that "God is light and in him there is no darkness" (1 Jn 1:5), and his "eyes are too pure to behold evil" (Hab 1:13). There's one thing we can be assured God does *not* in any sense do: evil.

The perfect love, holiness and justice revealed on the cross and attested to throughout Scripture must not be compromised or qualified. There is no non-Christlike streak in God. The fullness of God is revealed in Christ. God is decisively revealed nowhere else but in Christ.

How then are we to explain Isaiah 45:7 and Lamentations 3:37-38? This leads to my fourth point. If read in context, these passages are perfectly consistent with the biblical teaching that God "does not willing afflict, or grieve anyone." These passages simply do not teach that God is behind all good and evil, creating light and darkness and weal and woe whenever it comes to pass.[3]

The Isaiah passage is addressing the future deliverance of the children of Israel out of Babylon (Is 45:1-6). As a number of scholars have argued, the "light" and "darkness" of this passage refers to "liberation" and "captivity" (as in Is 9:2; Lam 3:2). The "weal" and "woe" refers to the Lord's plans to bless Israel and to curse Babylon. The passage is thus not suggesting that God's character is ambiguous, as though all darkness and all suffering in the world come from God. Rather it's suggesting that God's character is perfectly just, for he ultimately responds to injustice by bringing "darkness" and "woe" on those who perpetrate it.

Similarly, if read in context, Lamentations 3:37-38 does not suggest that the Lord brings about evil. Indeed, four verses earlier the same prophet taught that God "does not willingly afflict or grieve anyone" (Lam 3:33). This passage isn't speaking about God's activity *in general*; it's speaking specifically about prophecy. Both "good and bad" prophecies—prophecies about blessings and disaster—come "from the mouth of the Most High." As much as it grieves the Lord (see vv. 31-33), he is prophesying judgment on Israel because "the prisoners of the land are crushed under foot" and "human rights are perverted" (v. 34).

Far from suggesting that good and evil are part of God's sovereign plan, as blueprint theologians suggest, this passage highlights God's unequivocal goodness in moving *against* evil! Only when these passages are read in isolation from their specific literary and historical contexts do they lend support to the blueprint view that God is behind good and evil alike.

THE LORD TURNS THE KING'S HEART

> *The king's heart is a stream of water in the hand of the Lord; he turns it wherever he will.* (Prov 21:1)

Defenders of the blueprint theology sometimes argue that this passage teaches that everything government officials do is the result of the Lord turning their heart. In light of the hideous things many government officials have done (e.g., Hitler's program of ethnic cleansing), and in light of Scriptures that frequently depict God's outrage at government officials, we should seriously question this conclusion.

First, the genre of this passage is proverb. Hebrew proverbs often state general principles in unequivocal terms for emphasis. As we noted earlier (see variable five in chapter six), it was the Hebrew way of putting an exclamation point at the end of a teaching (Hebrew has no punctuation marks). We misinterpret proverbs if we understand them as universal laws.

For example, Proverbs 12:21 states: "No harm happens to the righteous, but the wicked are filled with trouble" (see also Prov 13:21, 25). If read as an unequivocal universal law, this passage is nonsense. History and our own experience demonstrate that righteous people frequently suffer great harm while wicked people often live in prosperity and peace. Scripture itself repeatedly makes this observation (e.g., the book of Job). Indeed, Jesus told his disciples to expect suffering (Jn 16:33). *As a general principle,* however, righteous living helps us avoid harm while wicked living will lead to trouble. The author states the principle in absolute terms to emphasize its importance.

Along similar lines Proverbs 22:6 states: "Train children in the right way, and when old, they will not stray." Over the years I have worked with disappointed parents who mistook this proverb as an unconditional promise of God, only to have it come back and bite them when their children strayed. As we all know, children have free will and often make poor choices, disregarding their upbringing. There is no risk-free parenting program! Nevertheless, it's very important—and thus stated in unequivocal terms—to train children in the right way.

So it's not advisable to interpret Proverbs 21:1 as an absolute law. The author is not suggesting that every decision made by every king throughout history was orchestrated by God. He is simply emphasizing God's general sovereignty over kings. Scripture contains examples of God steering the wicked intentions of kings toward his own end (e.g., 1 Chron 5:26; Is 10:5-6). But we read too much into this passage if we conclude that he uniformly controls everything leaders do.

Even when God "turns" the hearts of kings in the direction he desires, he doesn't *determine the nature of the heart* he turns, and this is my second point. People are free; thus they establish their own hearts and make their plans either in accordance with or against God's will (see chapter two). But even when they set themselves against God, he still "directs their steps" (Prov 16:9). With an infinite wisdom that has been anticipating their possible decisions from the beginning of time, God steers the way people live so that they (as much as possible) further his sovereign purposes for the world. He is always at work bringing good out of evil (Rom 8:28). But he doesn't *work the evil* he brings good out of.

THE LORD CREATES THE WICKED
FOR THE DAY OF TROUBLE

> The LORD has made everything for its purpose,
>
> even the wicked for the day of trouble. (Prov 16:4)

Some blueprint theorists cite this verse to support the conclusion that some people are created wicked for the purpose of being sent to hell ("the day of trouble"). In my estimation, this interpretation is extremely unlikely.

For one thing, this interpretation fundamentally conflicts with the truth that Christ is the definitive revelation of God and constitutes who we are before God. It also contradicts the revelation that God is love and Christ died for all people (Jn 3:16; 1 Jn 2:2; 4:8, 16). Finally, it reverses scriptural teaching that God does not willingly afflict or damn anyone (Lam 3:33; Ezek 18:30-32; 33:11; 1 Tim 2:4; 2 Pet 3:9).

Tragically, the blueprint interpretation changes the ultimate truth revealed in Christ into a penultimate truth. Beneath the unsurpassable love revealed on the cross we presumably find a more fundamental, non-Christlike revelation of God's character: God actually wills the damnation of people in opposition to what he reveals about himself on the cross. With laudable honesty, Calvin himself called this secret decree "horrible."[4]

Is it even intelligible to suggest that God creates wicked people just to damn them? Can we even conceive of a good God making people wicked, yet holding *them* responsible for the wickedness? Could God remain holy while doing this? Would a just God punish people for exhibiting the very character *he created them to have?* For my part, I don't know how to form an intelligible answer to these questions.

Fortunately, there is an alternative interpretation of Proverbs 16:4. This Scripture is using what scholars call "the language of moral order." God wisely designed creation such that good is (eventually) rewarded and evil (eventually) punished. In this sense the "purpose" for the wicked is found in the coming "day of trouble." It's significant to note that the Hebrew verb translated in the NRSV as "made" can be translated as "works out" (as in the NIV), an observation that confirms my interpretation. God steers the wickedness of agents so that their end eventually fits the moral order of the creation he wisely designed.

Consistent with this, the word translated as "purpose" can be translated as "answer." Hence, the meaning of the passage is that God works things out so that the end of the wicked "answers" their wickedness. They eventually reap what they sow. Thus we need not accept the nightmarish prospect of God creating people for the expressed purpose of having them suffer unending damnation.

Evil Intentions Used for Good

> Joseph said to his brothers . . . "now do not be distressed, or angry with yourselves, because you sold me here; for God sent me before you to preserve life."
> (Gen 45:4-5)

Joseph said to [his brothers], "Even though you intended to do harm to me, God intended it for good, in order to preserve a numerous people." (Gen 50:20)

Some argue that these two passages indicate that God orchestrated the evil intentions of Joseph's brothers in order to get him into Egypt. From this they conclude that there must be a divine reason behind every evil intention, allowing or ordaining it for a greater good. Is this a reasonable application of these passages? I don't believe so.

It is important to note that these passages don't suggest that God's decision to use the brothers' evil activity for good took place before creation or even before the brothers developed their own character traits. The passages only suggest that *at some point* God decided that it fit his sovereign purpose to steer the brothers' intentions in a certain manner. Had the brothers' moral character developed differently, God would have had in place a different plan to get Joseph and them into Egypt. Because we finite humans can't conceive of how God can accomplish his ends without coercion, some conclude that God must have planned the brothers' betrayal all along. But we have already seen the harm that occurs when we project our own limitations onto God and deny his unlimited intelligence and creative wisdom.

It's one thing for God to *use* the evil intentions of people who have freely chosen evil—such as Pharaoh, Judas and Joseph's brothers—but it's quite another thing for God to *predestine* people to have evil character or to steer people to evil against their will. Scripture never records God doing the latter, though it provides many instances of the former. There is no moral dilemma created by affirming God's sovereign right to use evil for his own purpose. But there is an insurmountable moral dilemma created if God sovereignly predetermines that certain people engage in evil.

On a closely related matter, some Christians suppose that Jesus' crucifixion counters the warfare worldview. Luke records an early Christian prayer that in part says:

Herod and Pontius Pilate, with the Gentiles and the peoples of Israel, gathered together against your holy servant Jesus . . . to do
whatever your hand and your plan had predestined to take place.
(Acts 4:27-28)

Earlier Peter had preached that Jesus was "handed over . . . according to
the definite plan and foreknowledge of God" and was crucified by law-
less people (Acts 2:23).

Do these statements mean that God predestined these individuals to
crucify the Messiah? No. To be sure, both passages clearly teach that God
decided ahead of time that Christ would be handed over and killed. This
much was predestined and foreknown. This much was part of his plan.
But the passages don't suggest that God predestined or foreknew who
would carry out his plan.

Again, some argue that it's impossible for God to guarantee a certain
outcome without guaranteeing the means to that outcome. If Jesus was
predestined to be crucified, they reason, then God had to predestine who
would do it. But there is absolutely no basis for this claim. Sociologists,
biologists, stock market analysts, insurance agents and military strategists
can predict group outcomes very accurately without being able to predict
individual behavior. Even so, God, who knows perfectly the probabilities
of all individual and group behavior, could send his son at the right time
to accomplish his plan (Rom 5:6; Gal 4:4). And God wouldn't have to
predestine any individuals to commit evil acts to ensure this.

We may conclude that God sometimes predestines events, but he
doesn't predestine individuals. He sometimes uses the evil intentions of
people to fulfill his predestined plans, but he doesn't predestine people
to have these evil intentions.

GOD CREATES MUTENESS, DEAFNESS AND BLINDNESS

The LORD said to [Moses], "Who gives speech to mortals? Who makes them
mute or deaf, seeing or blind? Is it not I, the LORD?" (Ex 4:11)

Some people argue that Exodus 4:11 teaches that all infirmities are specifically willed by God. Yet Jesus and the Gospel authors uniformly diagnosed muteness, deafness, blindness and other infirmities as directly or indirectly coming from the devil (see chapter two). Jesus demonstrated God's will for people by removing these infirmities. Is there a way of understanding this passage without contradicting the ministry of Jesus? Yes.

First, since Jesus is the center of the Christian faith, we must interpret the Exodus passage in the light of his ministry, *not the other way around.* In other words, this one Old Testament verse shouldn't render Jesus' explanation for evil penultimate. For example, some would suggest that while Satan is behind all infirmities, God ultimately controls Satan. In their view, this is how we should understand Exodus 4:11. Not only does this approach illegitimately reinterpret Jesus' entire ministry in the light of one rather obscure verse, it posits a rift between the Father (who supposedly controls Satan) and the Son (who opposes Satan). Indeed, it creates an irreparable duplicity in the Father himself: the Father's will is done by Satan, *and* the Father's will also is done by Jesus as he resists Satan. If we accept that God can't be divided or duplicitous, we must seek a different interpretation of the Exodus passage.

Second, it's very important to read the Exodus passage in context. Moses was arguing against God's decision to use him as his spokesperson on the grounds that he was "slow of speech and slow of tongue" (Ex 4:10). God was frustrated with Moses because he had just demonstrated that he could perform enough miracles to convince the Jewish elders that Moses was sent by God. Thus God used emphatic, unqualified language to establish the point that as Creator of the universe he could handle any and all obstacles in attaining his objective. In this context he rhetorically asked Moses, "Who gives speech to morals? Who makes them mute or deaf?" It's unlikely that the statement is meant to be taken as a metaphysical explanation of why people are deaf or mute.

Finally, notice what God does *not* say in this passage. God speaks of the human condition in *general* terms. He doesn't say that he picks and chooses which *individuals* will be born mute or deaf. He simply asserts that he is Creator of the kind of world in which some people become disabled.[5] The point of the statement is that Moses needed to know that the Creator was able to work around all obstacles in achieving his objectives. This verse does not teach that the Lord is the direct cause of every instance of these afflictions.

Along these same lines the central truth of the Old Testament is that there is one Creator God, not a multitude of conflicting gods. The Old Testament thus emphasizes that God, like an ancient Near Eastern monarch, is the *ultimate source* of everything, whether he wills it directly or not. The Lord is emphasizing this fact to reassure Moses that his speech impediment is no problem. But he is not thereby denying what later revelation will make clear; namely, infirmities such as muteness or blindness originate from Satan, and God wants to empower human mediators to free people from these afflictions.

GOD HARDENS PEOPLE'S HEARTS

> *There was not a town that made peace with the Israelites, except the Hivites;*
> *. . . all were taken to battle. For it was the Lord's doing to harden their hearts*
> *so that they would come against Israel in battle, in order that they might be*
> *utterly destroyed. (Josh 11:19-20)*

Some argue that passages which speak of God hardening human hearts (see also Ex 7:3; 10:1; 14:4; Deut 2:30; Rom 9:18) demonstrate that God controls everything, including people resistant to his declared intentions. He hardens whomever he wills, they argue. He could just as easily have softened their hearts, but for his own sovereign reasons he chose not to. Thus even the apparent conflict between God and Satan and rebellious humans is part of his sovereign will.

It's difficult to reconcile the notion that God hardens people's hearts so they won't believe with Jesus' unqualified love for the world. *When we see Christ*—hanging in love on the cross to reconcile us to himself—*we see the Father* (Jn 14:7-9). This self-sacrificial love is what God looks like. Christ is God's "exact imprint," his enfleshed icon (Heb 1:3; see also Col 1:15; 2 Cor 4:6). How is this revelation compatible with the frightful suggestion that God arbitrarily hardens people's hearts to keep them from coming to him?

Moreover, how do we reconcile a God who intentionally hardens people in damnable wickedness with the biblical teaching that God "does not willingly afflict, or grieve anyone" (Lam 3:33)? Can we reconcile this frightful idea with the consistent biblical teaching that God desires *everyone* to turn to him (Is 30:18; 65:2; Ezek 18:30-32; 33:11; Hos 11:7-9; Rom 10:21; 1 Tim 2:3-4; 2 Pet 3:9) and that evil flows from humans' own hearts (Mt 15:19; Lk 6:45)? There is no adequate answer to these questions. Fortunately, there is no reason to suppose that this is what these passages mean.

The root meaning of the Hebrew word translated "to harden" is "to strengthen." God hardens people by strengthening the resolve *they have formed in their own heart.* For example, six times Scripture says "the Lord hardened Pharaoh's heart" (Ex 9:12; 10:1, 20, 27; 11:10; 14:8). But it also notes that Pharaoh hardened his own heart seven times *before* the Lord took this action (Ex 7:13-14, 22; 8:15, 19; 32; 9:7). Similarly, centuries before God hardened the Canaanites' hearts (see Judg 11), he had been tolerating their freely chosen wickedness and hardness toward him (see Gen 15:16). The unsurpassable love of God strives to turn humans toward himself, but there is a point where they become hopeless (Gen 6:3-8; Rom 1:24-32). At this point God's strategy changes from trying to change them to using them in their wickedness for his own providential purposes.

God justly responds to people's wickedness by strengthening their resolve against him. In every instance where Scripture speaks of God hardening someone, it's an act of judgment in response to decisions these people had already made. God simply ensures that these rebels will do *what their own evil hearts desire* and not alter their course for ulterior motives. But it's altogether unwarranted to suppose that God unilaterally hardens people's hearts against himself in the first place—all the while pretending to offer them the hope of salvation! When God decides to harden someone's heart, we can be assured that God wishes it didn't have to be that way.

GOD ORDAINS PEOPLE TO BELIEVE

> *When the Gentiles heard this [preaching], they were glad and praised the word of the Lord, and as many as had been destined for eternal life became believers.* (Acts 13:48)

Luke tells us that some people were "destined for eternal life" before they heard the good news. Many assume that this "destiny" was given by God before the world began. If so, it seems we must accept the conclusion that God chose who would and would not be saved. This conclusion contradicts the finality of God's self-revelation in Christ and the universality of God's love. Hence, if there is another interpretation of this passage that avoids this contradiction, it seems it should be preferred.

Notice that Luke does not specify *when* the Gentiles who believed were "destined for eternal life." The text certainly doesn't require us to believe it was before they were born. It only requires us to accept that the Spirit of God had been preparing receptive hearts to accept the preaching that was soon coming their way. While God sometimes has to test people to find out what they'll do (e.g., Gen 22:12), when a person's heart turns a certain way God certainly knows it, even before these people manifest their heart in words or actions (Ps 139:1-4). On this basis the Lord could assure Paul before his missionary endeavor at Corinth that "there are many in this city who are my people" (that is, those whose hearts are open and who will therefore believe your message; Acts 18:10). So too, Lydia listened intently to Paul's gospel because the Lord had already "opened her heart" (Acts 16:14).

Those Gentiles who didn't resist the Spirit's work in their life were "ripe" for the message of Paul and Barnabas. In this sense they were already "destined for eternal life," and thus they accepted the good news when it was preached to them. But this doesn't mean that these Gentiles—in contrast to others?—were predestined from the foundation of the world to believe, or that Lydia had her heart "opened" from the foundation of the world. It simply means that they had been prepared by the Spirit ahead of time to receive the gospel and inherit eternal life.

This is probably how we ought to interpret Jesus' words when he tells certain Jews, "You do not believe, because you do not belong to my sheep. My sheep hear my voice. . . . [A]nd they follow me" (Jn 10:26-27). Jesus isn't implying that God unilaterally decided who would be his sheep, as some teach. And he certainly isn't suggesting that this matter was decided before any of these people were born. Jesus' words only imply that *at the time of his speaking* some people were sheep and therefore believed while others were not and therefore didn't believe. We create impossible problems for ourselves—such as how God can love all while predestining many to hell—when we go beyond what Scripture teaches.

JUDAS WAS DESTINED TO BETRAY JESUS

> *"But among you there are some who do not believe." For Jesus knew from the first who were the ones that did not believe, and who was the one that would betray him. (Jn 6:64)*

> *"I am not speaking of all of you; I know whom I have chosen. But it is to fulfill the scripture, 'The one who ate my bread has lifted his heel against me.' " (Jn 13:18)*

> *"While I was with them, I protected them in your name that you have given me. I guarded them, and not one of them was lost except the one destined to be lost, so that the scripture might be fulfilled." (Jn 17:12)*

Many Christians argue that the way Jesus speaks about Judas' betrayal shows that God predestines people to be saved or damned before they are born. If Jesus "knew from the first" Judas wouldn't believe, if it was prophesied in the Old Testament that he wouldn't believe, and if he was "destined to be lost," he couldn't have chosen differently. Several considerations argue against this conclusion, however.

First, when Scripture says Jesus knew "from the first" who would betray him, it does not imply that Jesus knew who would betray him from a time *before* Judas resolved to betray him. Indeed, the text doesn't say that Jesus knew this from the moment he chose Judas to be a disciple and certainly not from all eternity (as the blueprint view teaches). The Greek word *archē* can refer simply to the *start* of something (e.g., Mt 24:8; Mk 1:1; Jn 15:27; Acts 11:15) or can mean simply "early on" (e.g., Jn 8:11; Phil 4:5).

Second, many assume that when Jesus referred to Judas as one who was "destined to be lost," he meant that Judas was damned from before the beginning of time. However, the verse doesn't say this. The Greek translated as "destined to be lost" literally says "son of perdition," with no indication as to when Judas had become this. We only know that by the time Jesus said this Judas had freely made himself into a person fit for destruction.

Finally, Jesus tells us that Judas fulfilled Scripture, not that Judas was the one who *had* to fulfill Scripture. We have every reason to suppose that earlier on Judas could have chosen a different path. After all, earlier in Jesus' ministry Judas preached, healed people and exorcised demons along with the other disciples (Mk 3:14-15). It seems he was a genuine disciple. But as a free moral agent, Judas tragically chose a path of self-interest and self-destruction.

If Judas had gone down a different path, he wouldn't have fulfilled the prophecy of the Lord's betrayal. In this case the Lord would have found someone else with these character traits to fill this role. Or perhaps no one would have betrayed Jesus, and the passages that are now read as predicting his betrayal wouldn't be read as such.

Fulfilled prophecy. Many Christians assume that every Old Testament verse identified by the New Testament as being fulfilled in Jesus' ministry was a prediction that had to be fulfilled. But, as many scholars recognize, this is not an assumption shared by first century Jews.[6] Many times when the New Testament claims that Jesus fulfilled an Old Testament verse, it simply means that an aspect of Jesus' life serves as the supreme example of the point of the passage.

For example, when Matthew claimed that Jesus fulfilled Hosea 11:1 by entering and exiting Egypt as a child, he was not thereby claiming that Hosea *predicted* that the Messiah had to do this. The verse in Hosea is referring to Israel's flight from Egypt. There is no predictive quality to it, and it says nothing about the future Messiah. Yet there is a parallel between what happened to Israel and what happened to Jesus. Since Matthew wanted to demonstrate that Jesus is the founder of the new Israel, he simply notes one way in which Jesus' life parallels the history of Israel. Indeed, God's leading Israel safely out of Egypt can be seen as a prototype of Jesus' exodus from Egypt. In this sense Jesus' exodus "fulfills" the Old Testament exodus. If circumstances hadn't forced Jesus' family to go into Egypt, no one would have worried about the fulfillment of Hosea 11.

Another example demonstrates the use of "fulfillment" even more clearly. John says that Jesus was given sour wine on the cross to fulfill Scripture (Jn 19:28-29). He is referring to Psalm 69:21, in which David complains that his enemies "gave me poison for food, and for my thirst they gave me vinegar to drink." The Old Testament verse clearly predicts nothing. It simply describes David's mistreatment. John's point in saying Jesus "fulfilled" this verse was not that Jesus *had* to be given vinegar (or sour wine). It was only a way of noting that Jesus is the supreme example—the fulfillment—of servants of God like David who have been mistreated.

If we assume, as many conservative Christians do, that Psalm 69:12 was a prophecy Jesus had to fulfill, it becomes impossible to explain why Jesus was never given poison for food! Are we to believe that the second half of a sentence had to be fulfilled while the first half wasn't prophetic at all?

In this light, it seems most reasonable to conclude that no one *had* to betray Jesus, just as Jesus didn't *have* to come out of Egypt and no one *had* to give Jesus sour wine. In reference to Judas, the Old Testament passage that Jesus appeals to (Ps 41:9) has no inherent predictive quality to it. David is speaking about his betrayal by a close friend. No one would ever conclude ahead of time that the Messiah had to be betrayed on the basis of this verse. Yet, in the light of what was about to happen to Christ, we can understand his citing this verse to show that all instances of righteous people being betrayed are supremely illustrated in what Judas was about to do. And he cites his future betrayal and this parallel to assure his disciples that he is, in fact, the Messiah (Jn 13:19).

CONCLUSION

Though there are passages of Scripture that appear to contradict the warfare worldview, when examined closely, they don't. In each case an alternative, more plausible interpretation is available.

EPILOGUE

Why did Melanie's baby die in childbirth when, for all we know, in the next room a woman gave birth to a healthy baby she didn't want? Why did one person miraculously escape the terrorist attack on the World Trade Center when another arrived just in time to be incinerated? Why does a family who prays for protection lose their son in a car crash while others who never pray avoid crashes their entire life? In this book I have argued that there is no answer to such "why" questions. It's an impenetrable mystery.

Yet everything hangs on where we locate the mystery. Is it a mystery about God or about creation? If we accept Christ as our definitive picture of God, the answer must be the latter. Amidst the vast sea of things we cannot know, we *can* know that God looks like Jesus Christ, dying a god-forsaken death on the cross for rebellious sinners. While we can't begin to penetrate the complex factors that lie behind every event in world history, we can know God's attitude toward and purposes for us.

We have every reason to believe that the nightmarish aspects of life do not come from God. Christ reveals that the nightmarish aspects of life ultimately come from Satan, legions of fallen angels and people who are aligned with them. Evil things happen because of them, not God. Indeed, Christ revealed *God's* will by bringing relief and deliverance to those who suffered. Thus with our eyes fixed on Jesus, we have no reason to believe that God is secretly orchestrating the deaths of newborn infants, terrorist attacks on skyscrapers, fatal car crashes or any other instances of grotesque suffering. God is *not* to blame!

This is not to say that God doesn't use the evil intentions of people and fallen angels to further his own sovereign purposes. He certainly does. Indeed, here too Christ is our definitive guide, for God used the evil intentions of people and fallen angels to fulfill his mission to defeat the devil and reconcile us to himself (Acts 2:23; 1 Cor 2:7-8).

On a personal level, we can be assured that whatever happens to us, however nightmarish it may be, God is at work to turn the situation to our advantage (Rom 8:28). Among other things, he wisely uses suffering to build our character and strengthen our reliance on him. While we need not assume there is a divine purpose *leading to* our suffering, we can and must trust that there is a divine purpose that *follows from it.* Hence, our suffering is not meaningless.

In granting that God uses evil, however, we must take care not to compromise the supremacy of the revelation of God in Christ. This is done by those who imply that the evil intentions of agents and the resultant suffering are aspects of God's original plan for creation. Though God perfectly and eternally anticipates a response to each evil act, he does not will it. Indeed, evil intentions are evil precisely because they are *against* God's will. When we confuse God's will with the wills of fallen agents, the beauty of God revealed in Christ is inevitably compromised.

I believe that this truth is extremely important to remember when we are experiencing the painful arbitrariness of life. We are in a war zone, and everything hangs on our being able to identify who is fighting *against us* and who is fighting *for us.* The ultimate criteria for deciding what is and is not from God is Jesus Christ. If the one who died on the cross wouldn't have done it, you have every reason to assume an event is not from God or part of his will. Living with this Christ-centered perspective, we are freed from asking the unanswerable question of why life unfolds the particular way it does, and we are empowered to do something about it.

Of course, neither this nor any other theological perspective can give Melanie her child back. And neither this nor any other theological perspective can fully take away the pain of her loss. But by accepting the ambiguity of a war-torn creation and the clarity of God's beauty revealed in Christ, Melanie was able to rekindle her love for God and her passion for life. The painful ambiguity of life cannot crush one whose eyes are fixed on Jesus Christ. Next to this, nothing else really matters.

NOTES

Introduction: Why Did God Do This?
[1]The names and details of people involved in episodes taken from my own experience have been altered to preserve the anonymity of those involved.

Chapter 1: The Lie and the Truth
[1]On the concept of holiness, see R. Hodgson, "Holiness," in *Anchor Bible Dictionary*, ed. D. N. Freedman (New York: Doubleday, 1992), 3:237-54.

[2]See the groundbreaking study of W. M. Clark who successfully established that the concept of "the knowledge of good and evil" was about humans transgressing the divine-human boundary by trying to be morally autonomous from God. "Judgment in the Old Testament is ultimately a matter of God," he writes ("A Legal Background to the Yahwist's Use of 'Good and Evil' in Genesis 2—3," *Journal of Biblical Literature* 88 [1969]: 272). For an overview of various interpretations of "the knowledge of good and evil," see John Wenham, *Genesis*, Word Biblical Commentary (Waco, Tex.: Word, 1987), pp. 62-64. For a full treatment of the meaning and significance of the tree of the knowledge of good and evil and how it blocks God's central purpose for our lives—to be recipients and conduits of God's love—see my forthcoming book *Love and the Knowledge of Good and Evil*.

[3]It is worth noting that the Greek word *krinō* ("judgment") means "to separate." While we are forbidden to separate ourselves from and put ourselves above other people, as when we act as their judge, we are commanded to separate behaviors and events, as when we discern that the impact of an action is good or evil (Heb 5:14).

[4]See Terrence Fretheim, "Word of God," *Anchor Bible Dictionary*, ed. D. N. Freedman (New York: Doubleday, 1992), 6:961-68.

[5]Some Calvinists believe that God loves only the elect, at least to the point of wanting to save them. For several strict Calvinistic reflections on the love of God, see John MacArthur Jr., *The Love of God* (Dallas: Word, 1996); and D. A. Carson, *The Difficult Doctrine of the Love of God* (Wheaton, Ill.: Crossway, 2000). From my perspective the fundamental problem with this understanding is that it is not adequately Christocentric. Instead of reading all Scripture through the lens of Calvary, the Bible as a whole is read through the lens of a deterministic theological

system. Consequently, the revelation of God in Christ is not allowed to tell the whole story of God's relationship to humanity. The cross only reveals God's attitude toward *some* people (his elect). To all others, God's wrath is his definitive and permanent word.

Chapter 2: Evil and the Blueprint

[1]Generally, the strong form of the blueprint worldview represents classical Calvinism, while the weak form of the blueprint worldview represents certain forms of Arminianism. However, an increasing number of Arminians are denying that there is a specific divine reason behind what free agents do. In their view God foreknows all that will happen, but this foreknowledge doesn't empower him to *orchestrate* what comes to pass. The ultimate reason behind what free agents do, and thus the ultimate reason why things happen as they do insofar as they are influenced by free decisions, is found in agents, not in God. My critique of the blueprint worldview does not apply to this latter category of Arminians. Indeed, one could affirm everything I say about the warfare worldview and remain in this camp.

[2]For helpful assessments of the influence of Greco-Roman thought on early Christian theology, particularly its view of God, see W. Jaeger, *Early Christianity and Greek Paideia* (Cambridge, Mass.: Harvard University Press, 1961); J. C. McLelland, *God the Anonymous: A Study in Alexandrian Philosophical Theology* (Cambridge, Mass.: Philadelphia Patristic Foundation, 1976); R. Mortly, *From Word to Silence*, 2 vols. (Bonn: Peter Hanstein, 1986); J. Pelikan, *Christianity and Classical Culture: The Metamorphosis of Natural Theology in the Christian Encounter with Hellenism* (New Haven, Conn.: Yale University Press, 1993); J. Shiel, *Greek Thought and the Rise of Christianity* (New York: Barnes & Noble, 1963); and G. Watson, *Greek Philosophy and the Christian Notion of God* (Dublin: Columbia Press, 1996). Thomas Morris has effectively argued that the meaning of a "perfect being" is not self-evident. Rather, it is largely "a function of our intuitions concerning what properties are great-making properties" ("Perfect Being Theology," *Noûs* 21 [1987]: 22). See also Thomas Morris, *Our Idea of God: An Introduction to Philosophical Theology* (Downers Grove, Ill.: InterVarsity Press, 1991), pp. 25-45. My argument is that Hellenistic intuitions about what a perfect being should be like largely contradict the revelation of God in Jesus Christ, yet they have significantly influenced the church's thinking about God. For a full development of this thesis see Gregory A. Boyd, *The Myth of the Blueprint* (Downers Grove, Ill.: InterVarsity Press, forthcoming).

[3]For a contemporary defense of the classical view of God as timeless, see Paul Helm, "Divine Timeless-Eternity," in *God & Time, Four Views*, ed. Gregory E. Ganssle (Downers Grove, Ill.: InterVarsity Press, 2001), pp. 28-60. William Lane Craig has recently presented a definitive refutation of this perspective in his *Time and Eternity: Exploring God's Relationship to Time* (Wheaton, Ill.: Crossway, 2001).

[4]For an anthology of writings representative of "classical theism" on these points (including Augustine, Aquinas and Anselm), see Charles Hartshorne and W. Reese, *Philosophers Speak of God* (Chicago: University of Chicago Press, rpt 1976 [1953]), pp. 76-164.

[5]Augustine *The City of God*, Nicene and Post-Nicene Fathers, series 2 (hereafter NPNF2) (Peabody, Mass.: Hendrickson, 1994), 9:92.

[6]Augustine *Enchiridion*, Library of Christian Classics, ed. J. Baille, J. McNeil and H. P. Van Duren, trans. A. C. Outler (Philadelphia: Westminster Press, 1955), 7:400.

[7]Similarly, Augustine writes, "In their very act of [wicked people] going against [God's] . . . will, his will is thereby accomplished . . . for it would not be done without his allowing it—and surely his permission is not unwilling, but willing" (ibid., p. 389).

[8]According to Augustine, the victim "ought not to attribute [suffering] to the will of men, or of angels, or of any created spirit, but rather to His will who gives power to wills" (*City of God*, NPNF2, 10:93).

[9]Augustine, "The Free Choice of the Will," in *Fathers of the Church*, trans. R. P. Russell (Washington, D.C.: Catholic University Press of America), p. 59.

[10]John Calvin *Institutes of the Christian Religion* (trans. F. L. Battles) 1.16.2.

[11]Many blueprint theologians distinguish between (1) God's will and attitude toward evil events considered in their particularity, and (2) evil events considered as part of the whole of world history. Thus God may will and be pleased by things in terms of how they contribute to the good of the whole of world history, but not be pleased with them in terms of their particularity. Hence God may love and hate the same event. See, for example, John Piper, "Are There Two Wills in God? Divine Election and God's Desire for All to Be Saved," in *The Grace of God and the Bondage of the Will*, ed. Thomas Schreiner and Bruce Ware (Grand Rapids: Baker, 1995), 1:107-32. Nevertheless, it would still hold true in this theology that behind a "frowning providence God hides a smiling face," for however horrendous an event may be in its particularity, it nevertheless pleases God to allow it for the greater good.

[12]John Piper, "Why I Do Not Say, 'God Did Not Cause the Calamity, But He Can Use It for Good,'" Desiring God Ministries, September 17, 2001 <www.desiringgod.org>.

[13]The New Testament depicts Christ as embodying the wisdom of God in part because God outsmarted the devil in allowing him to orchestrate his crucifixion (1 Cor 2:1-8). On this, see chapter nine of my *God at War* (Downers Grove, Ill.: InterVarsity Press, 1996).

[14]For a fuller exposition of how the ministry of Jesus contradicts the blueprint worldview, see Boyd, *God at War*, pp. 171-237.

[15]To say that God does not *cause* or *specifically allow* events for a specific divine purpose is not to deny that God can perfectly *anticipate* evil events and wisely *respond* to fit them into a larger divine purpose. As I attempt to show in chapter nine, passages that are taken by some to teach that God brings about evil events can be better interpreted to teach that God wisely *makes use* of evil events.

[16]For a more developed exposition of John 9:1-5, see Boyd, *God at War*, pp. 231-34.

[17]Augustine *City of God* 22.1, NPNF2, pp. 479-80.

[18]Quoted in Walter Kaufman, ed., *Religion from Tolstoy to Camus* (New York: Harper & Row, 1961), pp. 137-44.

[19]For fuller discussions of this scriptural motif, see John Sanders, *The God Who Risks: A Theology of Providence* (Downers Grove, Ill.: InterVarsity Press, 1998); Clark Pinnock, *The Most Moved Mover* (Grand Rapids: Baker, 2001); and Gregory A. Boyd, *The God of the Possible* (Grand Rapids: Baker, 2000).

Chapter 3: Freedom and Risk

[1]Irenaeus, for example, says that "there is no coercion with God, but a good will is present with Him continually." (*Against Heresies* 5.37, Ante-Nicene Fathers, ed. Alexander Roberts and

James Donaldson [Peabody, Mass.: Hendrickson, 1994], 1:518.) See also *Epistle to Diognetus* 7.4, which states that God sent his son "as one who saves by persuasion, not compulsion, for compulsion is no attribute of God" (*The Apostolic Fathers: Greek Texts and English Translations of Their Writings*, ed. J. B. Lightfoot and J. R. Harmer, trans., ed. and rev. M. W. Holmes [Grand Rapids: Baker, 1992], p. 54). For a fuller discussion, see chapter one of my *Satan and the Problem of Evil: Constructing a Trinitarian Warfare Theodicy* (Downers Grove, Ill.: InterVarsity Press, 2001). I will develop the thesis that Augustine moved the church's theology from a warfare worldview to a blueprint worldview more fully in my book *The Myth of the Blueprint* (Downers Grove, Ill.: InterVarsity Press, forthcoming).

[2]In chapter seven I will discuss prayer as an aspect of our morally responsible say-so and as an important variable in conditioning what God does.

[3]C. E. Arnold, *Powers of Darkness: Principalities and Powers in Paul's Letters* (Downers Grove, Ill.: InterVarsity Press, 1992), p. 81. See the discussion in my *God at War* (Downers Grove, Ill.: InterVarsity Press, 1996), p. 181.

[4]For a detailed exposition of all this, see Boyd, *God at War*, chaps. 6-10. For a fuller discussion on the relationship between spiritual warfare and "natural" evil, see Boyd, *Satan and the Problem of Evil*, pp. 242-318.

Chapter 4: Complexity and War

[1]While a central point of the book of Job is to refute the popular reward-and-punishment theology of the ancient wisdom tradition, the book nevertheless depicts Job as more blessed after his trial than before (Job 42:10), in keeping with the wisdom tradition and even (ironically) confirming the words of Eliphaz in Job 5. John Gibson comments, "The tight equations of orthodoxy between good works and prosperity and, even more, between suffering and sin, had to go. But the author has no desire to deny that over large areas of life such equations still operated . . . the author of the Book of Job is not out to destroy the insights of the [wisdom] movement to which he belonged, but to reinstate them on a more mature and less naïve basis" (John Gibson, *Job* [Philadelphia: Westminster Press, 1985], p. 266).

[2]For example, in Matthew 8:5-13 a centurion is said to have requested a visit from Jesus. The parallel account in Luke 7:2-10 says it was elders sent by a centurion who requested the visit. There is no contradiction once we accept the ancient idea that an authority's delegates are an extension of himself.

[3]Gibson, *Job*, p. 265.

[4]On the word *kûn*, see R. L. Harris, Gleason L. Archer and Bruce K. Waltke, *Theological Wordbook of the Old Testament* (Chicago: Moody Press, 1980), 1:433-34.

[5]For introductory works on chaos theory, see James Gleick, *Chaos: Making a New Science* (New York: Penguin, 1987); J. Holte, ed., *Chaos: The New Science; Nobel Conference XXVI* (Lanham, Md.: University Press of America, 1993); G. Nicolis and I. Prigogine, *Exploring Complexity: An Introduction* (New York: W. H. Freeman, 1989); I. Prigogine and I. Stengers, *Order Out of Chaos: Man's New Dialogue with Nature* (Toronto: Bantam, 1984); and D. Ruelle, *Chance and Chaos* (Princeton, N.J.: Princeton University Press, 1991). Closely related to chaos theory is the newly emerging complexity theory. For introductions, see R. Lewin, *Complexity: Life at the Edge of Chaos* (New York: Macmillan, 1992) and M. M. Waldrop, *Complexity: The Emerging Science*

at the Edge of Order and Chaos (New York: Simon & Shuster, 1992). In *Satan and the Problem of Evil* ([Downers Grove, Ill.: InterVarsity Press, 2001], chaps. 5-7) I argue that contemporary evangelical thought in general has not adequately integrated the insights offered in these fields or the field of quantum physics with our understanding of divine providence.

[6]For a fuller discussion, see chapter three of my *God at War* (Downers Grove, Ill.: InterVarsity Press, 1996).

[7]Though the psalmist hyperbolically emphasizes Yahweh's supremacy to the point that he depicts him as simply sporting with Leviathan (Ps 104:26).

[8]Fredrik Lindström, *God and the Origin of Evil: A Contextual Analysis of Alleged Monistic Evidence in the Old Testament*, trans. F. H. Cryer (Lund: Gleerup, 1983), 154.

[9]Ibid., p. 156.

[10]J. C. L. Gibson, "On Evil in the Book of Job," in *Ascribe to the Lord: Biblical and Other Studies in Memory of Peter C. Craigie*, ed. L. Eslinger and G. Taylor, JSOT Sup. 67 (Sheffield: Sheffield Academic Press, 1988), p. 412. See also J. C. L. Gibson, *Job* (Philadelphia: Westminster Press, 1985), pp. 225-56; and *Language and Imagery in the Old Testament* (Peabody, Mass.: Hendrickson, 1998), pp. 99-103. Other scholars who share this general perspective are O. Keel, *Jahwes Entgegung an Job*; FRLANT 121 (Göttingen: Vandenhoeck & Ruprecht, 1978); J. Day, *God's Conflict with the Dragon and the Sea* (Cambridge: Cambridge University Press, 1985), pp. 62-87, and T. Mettinger, "The God of Job: Avenger, Tyrant, or Victor?" in *The Voice from the Whirlwind: Interpreting the Book of Job*, ed. L. G. Perdue and W. C. Gilpin (Nashville: Abingdon, 1992), pp. 39-49.

[11]On the centrality of this motif in Scripture, see my forthcoming *Love and the Knowledge of Good and Evil* (Downers Grove, Ill.: InterVarsity Press, forthcoming).

Chapter 5: Omnipotence and Two Variables

[1]"After" in this sentence is logical, not temporal. Though God often times tested people to see what they would do (e.g., Gen 22:12; Deut 8:2; 13:1-3; 2 Chron 32:31), we need not conceive of God as having to wait until a person makes a decision to assign a reason for it. Because God is infinitely intelligent, he can perfectly anticipate every *possibility* from all eternity as though it were a certainty and thus plan a perfect response to it from all eternity—if he so chooses.

A word should be said about the "open theism" debate that has generated so much heat in evangelical circles in the last decade. Open theists hold that insofar as God gives freedom to agents, the future is composed of possibilities that are known by God as such. This conflicts with the traditional view that God is eternally certain of all that will come to pass, including the decisions of free agents. Yet if both sides grant that God is infinitely intelligent and that he gave free will to agents, *nothing of any practical significance hangs in the balance of this debate* as it concerns God's foreknowledge. For if God is infinitely intelligent, there is no practical difference between anticipating a possibility as opposed to a certainty. It is only because *we humans* are limited in intelligence that we can't anticipate possibilities as perfectly as we can certainties, for we have to "spread our intelligence out," as it were, to cover the various possibilities. By contrast, a God of unlimited intelligence could attend to every future possibility *as though* it were the *only* possibility that could come to pass (i.e., as though it were foreknown as a certainty). Only when we unwittingly assume that God is *limited in intelligence like us* do we worry that he loses anything in terms of providential control by anticipating possibilities as opposed to certainties. Critics of open theism repeatedly charge it holds to an anthropomorphized deity (that is, a deity limited like humans) who has to worry about the future. Ironically, the criticism itself presupposes an anthropomorphic God. For an overview of various perspectives on divine foreknowledge, see P. Eddy and J. Bilbey, eds., *Divine Foreknowledge: Four Views* (Downers Grove, Ill.: InterVarsity Press, 2001).

[2]In my view this is how we should interpret Scripture's declaration that God can't do some things (e.g., lie, be tempted, be unfaithful, be evil; 2 Tim 2:13; Jas 1:13). Given that he is the kind of God he is, he can't be other than he is for the exact same reason a triangle can't be a circle.

[3]For a fuller exposition, see Gregory A. Boyd, *Satan and the Problem of Evil* (Downers Grove, Ill.: InterVarsity Press, 2001), esp. chaps. 6-7.

[4]The "laws" of nature are simply descriptions of the regularity of nature. In the present context, they describe the rules humans count on in order to relate to other people. God doesn't literally break any laws when he intervenes in the world. He just suspends the ordinary rules. For a classic discussion on the need for regularity in nature for agents to relate to one another in morally responsible ways, see C. S. Lewis, *The Problem of Pain* (New York: Macmillan, 1945), pp.17-23.

I should also note that other philosophers have postulated a number of things that are required of nature if the Creator wants to achieve certain objectives. For example, some have argued that nature must not only be stable but must involve an element of indeterminacy, such as we find in quantum mechanics, if the cosmos is to produce free agents. See, for example, R. J. Russell, "Quantum Physics in Philosophical and Theological Perspective," in *Physics, Philosophy and Theology: A Common Quest for Understanding*, ed. R. J. Russell, W. R. Stoeger and G. V. Coyne (Notre Dame, Ind.: Notre Dame University Press, 1988). Others have argued that at every level the world must contain an element of indeterminacy to remain distinct from God (e.g., John Polkinghorne, *Science and Creation* (Boston: Shambhala, 1988), and *Quarks, Chaos & Christianity* (New York: Crossroad, 1996.) Similarly, some have argued that indeterminism in nature allows for novelty and generates forms of life that otherwise could not be generated. See, for example, John Polkinghorne, *Quarks*, p. 40; D. Bartholomew, *God of Chance* (London: SCM Press, 1984); and A. Peacock, *Creation and the World of Science* (Clarendon: Clarendon Press, 1979).

Chapter 6: Prayer and Ambiguity

[1]For an excellent discussion of the biblical material depicting God as allowing us to influence him and thereby influence what comes to pass, see John Sanders, *The God Who Risks* (Downers Grove, Ill.: InterVarsity Press, 1998), pp. 53-66, 100; and Terrence Fretheim, "Divine Dependence Upon the Human: An Old Testament Perspective," *Ex Auditu* 13 (1997): 1-13.

[2]John Wesley, quoted approvingly in P. E. Billheimer, *Destined for the Throne* (Minneapolis: Bethany House, 1975), p. 51. In my estimation this little work remains one of the all-time classics on prayer. Others who express similar convictions are Brother Andrew and S. D. Williams, *And God Changed His Mind Because His People Prayed* (Grand Rapids: Baker, 1999); Watchman Nee, *What Shall This Man Do?* (London: Victory Press, 1961), and *The Prayer Ministry of the Church* (Anaheim, Calif.: Living Stream Ministry, 1995).

[3]Paul Billheimer, *Destined for the Throne*, pp. 51-52. Watchman Nee has a similar understanding of prayer. "The water of divine deliverance," he writes, "depends upon the provision of human ditches" (*What Shall This Man Do?* p. 147).

[4]I responded by wondering aloud why no one had ever thought of doing this before him.

[5]The oversimplification and overgeneralization of this second variable is especially prevalent within the Word-Faith or Positive Confession movement. In its more extreme version people are taught that if they have enough faith, they will be healed and financially prosperous. Hence, if a person is not healed or wealthy, it's because they lack faith.

[6]For several scientific studies that seem to confirm a connection between the effectiveness of prayer and the persistence and number of people praying, see L. Dossey, *Healing Words: The Power of Prayer and the Practice of Medicine* (San Francisco: HarperSanFrancisco, 1993); D. Matthews, *The Faith Factor: Proof of the Healing Power of Prayer* (New York: Viking, 1998); and T. Hudson, "Measuring the Results of Faith," in *Hospitals and Health Networks* 70, no. 18 (1996). Of related interest see B. Epperly, "To Pray or Not to Pray: Reflections on the Intersection of Prayer and Medicine," *Journal of Religion and Health* 34 (1995): 141-48.

[7]Walter Wink, *Engaging the Powers: Discernment and Resistance in a World of Domination* (Minneapolis: Fortress, 1992), p. 310.

[8]Ibid., p. 311.

[9]Ibid.

[10]On the Lord's council of gods, see Gregory A. Boyd, *God at War* (Downers Grove, Ill.: InterVarsity Press, 1996), pp. 129-34.

[11]See, for example, J. M. Templeton and R. L. Herrman, *The God Who Would Be Known: Revelations of the Divine in Contemporary Science* (Philadelphia: Templeton Foundation Press, 1989); H. Margenau and R. A. Varghese, eds. *Cosmos, Bios, Theos: Scientists Reflect on Science, God, and the Origins of the Universe, Life, and Homo Sapiens* (LaSalle, Ill.: Open Court, 1992); R. J. Russell, et al., eds., *Physics, Philosophy and Theology: A Common Quest for Understanding* (Notre Dame, Ind.: University of Notre Dame Press, 1988); G. L. Schroeder, *The Hidden Face of God: How Science Reveals the Ultimate Truth* (New York: Free Press, 2001); *The Science of God: The Convergence of Scientific and Biblical Wisdom* (New York: Simon & Shuster, 1997); and Stanley Jaki, *The Road of Science and the Ways of God* (Chicago: University of Chicago Press, 1978).

Chapter 7: Life and Hope

[1]See, for example, Dallas Willard, *Hearing God: Developing a Conversational Relationship With God* (Downers Grove, Ill.: InterVarsity Press, 1999); L. Cunningham, *Is That Really You, God?* (Grand Rapids: Chosen Books, 1984); Gary Friesen, *Decision Making and the Will of God* (Sisters, Ore.: Multnomah Press, 1980).

[2]It is because we can't know the vast complexity of variables that lie behind people's decisions and the circumstances they find themselves in that we can't ever judge another person (Mt 7:1-5; Jas 4:11-12). Our only job is to love them. We can only offer wise and loving advice—or confrontation—when we are in relationship with others and thus know something about the complexity of their life. I develop this further in my forthcoming book *Love and the Knowledge of Good and Evil.*

Chapter 8: Mercy and Hardening

[1]No one prior to Augustine, other than the dualistic and deterministic Manichaeans (Augustine was a Manichaean prior to his conversion to Christianity) read Romans 9 in a determin-

istic fashion. In my forthcoming book *The Myth of the Blueprint* (Downers Grove, Ill.: InterVarsity Press) I will argue that Augustine's own reading of Romans 9 as well as his entire blueprint theology was very indebted to Manichaeism, Stoicism and Neo-Platonism.

[2]For a much more thorough refutation of the blueprint interpretation of Romans 9, see Paul Eddy, *A Flexible Sovereignty: The Case Against the Calvinist Interpretation of Romans 9* (publication pending). I am very indebted to Dr. Eddy for much of the material I put forth on Romans 9.

[3]E.g., Gen 12:2-3; 18:18; 22:18; Ps 67:1-2; Is 2:2-4; 55:5; 61:9-11; 66:19-20; Jer 3:17; Rom 4:12-18.

Chapter 9: Providence and Control

[1]This list is of course by no means exhaustive. For my response to other passages, see Gregory A. Boyd, *Satan and the Problem of Evil* (Downers Grove, Ill.: InterVarsity Press, 2001), pp. 394-416.

[2]Beza's teaching is illustrative. "Without [God's] eternal and changeless decree nothing is done anywhere by anyone either universally or specially, not even excepting those things which are evil and accordingly detestable; although not as decreed by an ever good and righteous God but as happening through Satan and other evil instruments" (H. Heppe, ed., *Reformed Dogmatics*, ed. E. Bizer, trans. G. T. Thomson, rev. ed. [Grand Rapids: Baker, 1978], pp. 142-43). How God decrees all things, including evil, while evil does not occur "as decreed by an ever good and righteous God" is not explained. Again Beza writes, "Nothing happens anyhow or without God's most righteous decree, although God is not the author of or sharer in any sin at all . . . at the time when He applies the devil or wicked men in achieving some work, whom He afterwards justly punishes, He Himself none the less effects His holy work well and justly. . . . When from eternity God decreed whatever was to happen at definite moments, He at the same time also decreed the manner and way which He wished it thus to take place to such extent, that even if some flaw is discovered in a second cause, it yet implies no flaw or fault in God's eternal counsel" (ibid., pp. 144-45). How God can eternally decree flaws while being flawless or justly punish the devil and wicked people for doing what he infallibly decreed they do is never explained. It is simply asserted.

[3]See Gregory A. Boyd, *God at War* (Downers Grove, Ill.: InterVarsity Press, 1997), pp.149-52.

[4]"The decree is dreadful (Latin, *horribile*) I confess" (John Calvin *Institutes of the Christian Religion* 3.3.7, The Library of Christian Classics 21, ed. J. T. McNeill, trans. F. L. Battles [Philadelphia: Westminster, 1960], p. 955). Calvin is explicit in affirming that God is the author of the reprobate disposition of those who are damned. Yet he insists, "Though I should confess a hundred times that God is the author of it—which is very true—yet they [the reprobate] do not promptly cleanse away the guilt that, engraved upon their consciences, repeatedly meets their eyes" (ibid., p. 951). God authors and decrees that people do evil, and yet God is holy for decreeing it while the people are guilty for doing what he decrees (see footnote 1).

[5]Terrence Fretheim, *Exodus*, Interpretation (Louisville, Ky.: John Knox Press, 1991), p. 72.

[6]See, for example, J. Sawyer, *Prophecy and the Biblical Prophets*, rev. ed. (New York: Oxford University Press, 1993), pp. 142-46; John Sanders, *The God Who Risks* (Downers Grove, Ill.: InterVarsity Press, 1998), pp. 133-34; John Goldingay, *Models for Interpretation of Scripture* (Grand Rapids: Eerdmans, 1995), pp. 122-27, 146-48.

Scripture Index